IT'S BETTER TO
BITE YOUR
TONGUE THAN
EAT YOUR
WORDS

Other Books by Mike Bechtle

IT'S BETTER TO
BITE YOUR TONGUE THAN EAT YOUR WORDS

The No-Regrets Guide to Better Conversations

DR. MIKE BECHTLE

Revell

a division of Baker Publishing Group
Grand Rapids, Michigan

© 2022 by Mike Bechtle

Published by Revell
a division of Baker Publishing Group
PO Box 6287, Grand Rapids, MI 49516-6287
www.revellbooks.com

Printed in the United States of America

Library of Congress Cataloging-in-Publication Data
Names: Bechtle, Mike, 1952– author.
Title: It's better to bite your tongue than eat your words : the no-regrets guide to better conversations / Dr. Mike Bechtle.
Description: Grand Rapids, MI : Revell, a division of Baker Publishing Group, 2022.
Identifiers: LCCN 2021027539 | ISBN 9780800737887 (paperback) | ISBN 9780800741419 (casebound) | ISBN 9781493434282 (ebook)
Subjects: LCSH: Attitude (Psychology) | Cognitive balance. | Conversation. | Interpersonal relations.
Classification: LCC BF327 .B44 2022 | DDC 158.1—dc23
LC record available at https://lccn.loc.gov/2021027539

Baker Publishing Group publications use paper produced from sustainable forestry practices and post-consumer waste whenever possible.

22 23 24 25 26 27 28   7 6 5 4 3 2 1

To Elena.
God handcrafted you
and designed you for his purpose.
When he finished, he said,
"Wow! I did *so good* on that one!"
Your uniqueness is why I treasure you.
You have given me great joy
simply because you're *you*!

Contents

Part 3 Inside-Out Communication 165

The Power
of Being Yourself

Be yourself. Everyone else is already taken.

Oscar Wilde (attributed)

This book is designed for two types of people:

1. Those who hesitate to speak up—and then think, *I wish I had said* . . . after most conversations.
2. Those who speak quickly without thinking—and then think, *I wish I hadn't said* . . . after most conversations.

Which one are you? There's a good chance you're both. We've all had regrets at times about things we should or shouldn't have said. It might be so common for you that you feel like you could never change.

Here's the good news: *you can change.*

That's what this book will help you do. You'll learn practical skills for building your conversational confidence, speaking up when your words could be helpful, and biting your tongue when your words could be hurtful. You'll also master actionable ideas for streamlining your communication skills in every situation.

I've lived this journey myself, and I know what those regrets at the end of conversations feel like. I'd wish I could go back and say things differently, but the damage had been done. I felt like I didn't have what it took to be an effective communicator. My lack of communication skills seemed to be part of who I was, and I would never find freedom.

But that freedom sure sounded attractive, and the desire for it kept dropping into my mind. That's when I began a journey to see if there might be hope for change.

On that journey, I discovered I didn't have to change my personality or temperament and pretend to be someone I wasn't. The process of change involved a series of simple, realistic steps that would lead to success. This success wouldn't happen *in spite of* who I really was but *because of* who I was. The "real me" turned out to be the very thing that would allow me to communicate with confidence.

It will happen for you as well. Your uniqueness will become your "superpower." You get to be completely "you"—and I'll help you become the best version of you possible.

You'll have "regret-free" conversations with everyone you meet!

Your Conversational Workout Plan

What if everyone could read your thoughts—all the time?

There's a gym near my house where everyone wears a heart rate monitor while they're in exercise classes. There are chest straps provided by the club, and these monitors help people exercise in the ideal range for their fitness goals based on their age and current physical condition. Charts on the wall give the best numbers to strive for, and they're color-coded to make it easy. The staff also helps you determine which color zone is appropriate for reaching your goals.

10

To make it even easier, there are large monitors on the walls that connect wirelessly to the sensors, and these display your numbers. Your box on the screen also changes color based on what zone you're in. You can change the color of your box by putting in more or less effort. You can see if you're in your "zone" from anywhere in the class area of the gym.

It's really clever. It's really helpful. And it's really public. Yes, you can see your own numbers and colors, but so can everyone else—and you can see theirs. If you have the slightest competitive bone in your body, it's hard not to compare. If someone else is doing better than you, you'll be either motivated or intimidated. If you're doing better than someone else, you might look at them and think, *What a slacker!*

Let's take this idea out of the gym and apply it to our interactions with others. What if there was a screen on the wall during every conversation or meeting, color-coded to show what people were really thinking or feeling? Everybody, including you, might be trying to look engaged and interested in a discussion, but people could glance at the screen to find the truth about your thoughts.

Green box: you're comfortable, engaged, and agreeing with what people are saying.

Blue box: you're bored and disengaged.

Red box: you have strong feelings against what's being discussed (but might not say anything out loud).

Yellow box: you just want everybody else to shut up so you can give your opinion.

White box: you're mentally on vacation in the Bahamas.

Black box: you've reached your limit—and nobody better block your way to the door.

That's what goes on behind the scenes in every conversation. Some people are just OK with it and can participate in the conversation without effort. But others struggle to express themselves; they really want to say something, but they don't have the courage. When they finally do speak up, it comes out wrong, and the other participants in the conversation don't understand or might be offended. Ten minutes after the conversation is over, they think of exactly what they should have said—and how they should have said it.

If that sounds like you, that's probably why you picked up this book. During conversations, you might feel like you're in a washing machine. Words and ideas swirl around you, and you're worried about drowning. You want to feel confident in your communication but seem to be lacking some of the basics of how to speak up appropriately and effectively. The words you want to say just disappear (like that one sock hiding behind the dryer).

You're not just hoping to *survive* but *thrive*. You wish you could just enjoy every conversation without worrying about how you're coming across. Is that possible? Absolutely—and I can promise it's even easier than you might think. You won't have to become bolder and more outgoing or more analytical or logical, turning into someone you're not.

The secret is to be completely you. Your uniqueness is how you'll make it happen, and we'll explore the process together.

Speak Up or Shut Up?

When it comes to communication, most people divide the world into two broad categories:

1. People who tend to be passive.
2. People who tend to be aggressive.

You might say, "That's not fair. I'm not in either category. I'm right in the middle." Unfortunately, that makes you passive-aggressive.

Let's try a different approach.

One group includes people who want to be *compassionate* in their communication. They focus on how their thoughts and words are impacting the other person, and they tend to hold back if they think they might hurt someone. They choose their words carefully so they meet the needs of the listener. They don't want to be misunderstood, so they usually don't speak until they've completely formulated their thoughts and ideas. This often means they don't say anything at all.

Another group includes people who seem to be *confident* in their communication. They share their opinions easily and always believe they know the right thing to say. They think quickly and articulate their thoughts without hesitation. If they disagree with someone, they just say so. They're more concerned about expressing their ideas well than how the other person receives those words. They can be brutally honest and even hurtful to others, and not even realize it.

Compassionate people ask, "Why can't I be more confident and have the courage to speak up when it's appropriate?" Confident people wonder, "What I'm saying is so obvious and logical; why won't people just listen to me?"

All of us could use a communication tune-up. We think that if we could just find the right tips and techniques, we'd be more effective in connecting with others. But everybody is different, and we all need different things. There is no "one-size-fits-all" solution.

Am I Enough?

When we aren't getting the results we want in life, it's easy to blame ourselves.

I weigh too much because I don't have enough discipline.
I worry too much because I'm just wired that way.

My house or office or car is messy because I'm just a
  messy person.
I don't make enough money, so I don't have as much value
  as other people.

In other words, we feel inadequate. We've tried to fix these
things in the past but keep going back to our old patterns. The
more it happens, the more we lose hope of permanent change.
We think, *This is just who I am, so I'll always be this way.*

When that's our mindset, it leaks into every area of our life—
including our relationships. We try to communicate effectively
with people, but it never quite works. Maybe we get discouraged when we don't stand up for ourselves and others. Maybe
we think we're communicating clearly, but people just aren't
getting it.

Nobody else seems to be having these problems, so we assume we're the problem. Whenever we compare ourselves with
others, we come up short. We believe we're not enough, and
we wonder where we can find a solution that will finally work.

So we go shopping for books and seminars to help us fill in
the gaps in our communication. We take assertiveness training
to be more forceful. We read books on sensitivity to become
more sensitive to others. But somehow it feels as artificial as an
aluminum Christmas tree. All of the advertisements for those
classes feature "before and after" stories of great success. "Just
sign up for this course, and you'll be successful."

We sign up and do exactly what they say. When it doesn't
work, we assume it's our own fault. The course worked for
everyone else, right? So the problem must be us: we didn't try
hard enough or we weren't disciplined enough. It reinforces
what we already believe—that we're the problem—and we spiral downward into a growing sense of inadequacy.

Is there hope? Absolutely—but it doesn't come from changing
who you are. Your uniqueness isn't the problem, *it's the solution.*

Why You're a Masterpiece

I'm writing this from a hotel room in Lancaster, California. It's a clean, simple room with the basics: a bed, a desk, a TV, and a microwave.

There's a painting on the wall. It's an abstract combination of shapes and colors. It's big and has an even bigger gold frame. I'm sure it's just a print, and there's a piece of glass covering it.

Now, I'm not an expert on art. But I think good art is supposed to capture your emotions. It catches your eye when you see it, and you interact with the painting in an emotional way. In other words, it moves you.

I'm not being moved by this painting. It's colorful, but I'm not sure what it represents. I'm not tempted to pull it off the wall and sneak it into my car.

That got me thinking. I don't know how many nights I've spent in hotel rooms in my life, but I'm sure it's in the thousands. Fancy hotels, cheap hotels, and everything in between. In all those nights, I can't think of a time when I've noticed a painting. I'm sure there was one in almost every room, but I didn't notice. They didn't grab me. But they didn't irritate me, either.

I wonder if hotels buy these paintings in bulk and use them to decorate their rooms to set the tone and make them feel "homey." By hanging nondescript art, they won't offend anyone—and don't have to worry about people stealing it.

I also wonder if the artist feels bad knowing that their artwork is so bland nobody would notice it or steal it. (But then again, if the artist gets a little commission for every print that's purchased, having the pieces in thousands of hotels might ease the pain.)

If I take that piece of hotel art to an art museum and put it on the wall, it will look out of place. But if the purpose is to set a tone for the room, it does its job well. It makes the room feel comfortable. If that's the purpose, it's the perfect painting for the wall.

It's a "masterpiece" in fulfilling its purpose.

Kind of like you. You're unique. There's nobody else like you. There's a purpose for your life that nobody else can fulfill. *If you fulfill that purpose, your life is a masterpiece.*

If you compare your life with somebody else's masterpiece, you're trying to fulfill their purpose, not yours. When that happens, you'll probably feel like a stick figure drawing next to a Rembrandt.

It's human nature to compare ourselves with others. Without even trying, we see someone we think is more attractive and wish we could look like them. If they're smarter or more articulate, we feel dumb and tongue-tied. If they're more outgoing, we think we could build better relationships if we were an extrovert. If they're more thoughtful and reflective, we might think we're not deep enough. Whatever it is, we're struggling, and we think they're not.

We often use other people as the standard to measure our value. It's like a cheetah feeling inferior when it sees an eagle flying overhead because it's stuck on the ground. If the eagle made that same comparison, it could be discouraged because it can't run that fast when it's moving on land.

"That's crazy," you say. "The thing that makes an eagle so majestic is its ability to soar through the sky. The cheetah is amazing because of its speed. They don't try to become something they're not; they're just being themselves and doing it really well."

That's the point. They're not comparing; they're just being themselves. Their value comes from their uniqueness. That's the foundation for this book. You don't have to try hard to become a masterpiece; you already are, just because you're *you*. You just need to recognize that it's true, then learn what to do with it.

Don't be somebody else. It robs the world of your uniqueness. Be you. Make your own unique contribution. Quit comparing yourself to others.

Be the best "you" you can be, and the world will see a work of art. When you're a masterpiece, you don't have to pretend to be more confident or more compassionate with others. You get to be *you*, and you become your own secret weapon for success.

The Key to Effective Communication

"That sounds good," you say. "But I'm not there yet. Even if I believe I'm a masterpiece, how does that translate into my relationships every day?"

When your relationships aren't working the way you'd like them to, you feel like you need to change. If you feel inadequate, you assume everybody thinks the same thing about you. If they're all feeling it (though the truth is almost no one does), you believe it must be true. So you experiment with different ways of connecting:

- You want others to see you as confident and strong, so you overcompensate and try to act more aggressive or assertive.
- You want others to feel good about you, so you become a people pleaser. You give in and give up, never sharing your true opinions or desires in order to keep people from being disappointed in you.
- You see others who appear strong and aggressive, but it feels obnoxious to you. You don't want to be like that, so you become terminally nice.
- You always seem to say the wrong thing at the wrong time in the wrong way, and it's discouraging.

Anytime you try to apply random techniques you hear about, you'll be frustrated when they don't work. "They worked well for others, so why don't they work well for me?" you ask.

Because you're not them; *you're you*.

The only effective, lasting solutions will be the ones that capitalize on your uniqueness. The more the solution fits your unique temperament, the more it will be a natural part of who you are. You'll be working out of your core, so your solutions will be completely customized. They won't be contrived or fake, like wearing clothes that are three sizes too big or too small. Instead of an off-the-shelf approach, you can design one that's been professionally tailored to exactly match who you are.

There's even better news: effective communication is a skill you can learn. You can stay true to yourself, which makes the process a natural extension of who you are. You'll be creating your own "tips and techniques" because they'll be generated organically instead of pasted on from the outside.

Once you gain this skill, you won't have to pretend to be courageous; you'll develop confidence and courage from the inside. You won't have to pretend to be compassionate; it will come naturally, which allows you to make a genuine impact. You still get to be "you"—but you can become a *better* you by applying some simple principles and practices.

It doesn't take forever, either. You'll spend the rest of your life practicing and honing your skills, but you can take steps *immediately* that lead to noticeable results. Each step gives you a new tool you can use right away to communicate effectively. Over time, you'll develop the perfect blend of *confidence* and *compassion* in every relationship. Your uniqueness becomes your superpower for connecting with others, and you'll be able to communicate without regret.

Where We're Headed

That's the journey we'll be taking together. We'll take a series of small steps to improve our communication skills, practicing each one until it becomes familiar before moving to the next.

You're not going to be forced out of your comfort zone to try things that are uncomfortable and threatening. We'll simply stick our toes over the edge to experiment, then practice for a while until it becomes part of our comfort zone. We won't rush through the process. This is a slow-cooked meal, not a microwave snack.

Little steps are building blocks for big results. We never reach perfection, but we can always grow. Eventually we'll arrive at a place where we can be ourselves, capitalizing on our uniqueness to connect well with others. We won't be anxious about how others perceive us; we'll just be ourselves—and it will be enough.

What's the payoff? Here are the outcomes you can expect as you practice the advice in the following chapters:

- You'll know how to communicate without stress or intimidation.
- You'll be able to stand up for yourself without being obnoxious.
- You'll get the respect you deserve without demanding it.
- You'll know how to respond in the moment instead of later.
- You'll be able to stand up for others who can't stand up for themselves.
- You'll learn how to pick your battles and avoid conflict with grace.
- You'll be able to confront effectively because you care.
- You'll know the difference between aggressiveness and assertiveness.
- You'll be able to use your emotions as fuel for genuine connection.
- You'll learn to keep from blaming yourself for mistakes.

- You'll be less critical of other people—and yourself.
- You'll say things to people you never would have said before.
- You'll become a world-class listener—not to impress, but because you want to understand.
- You'll end conversations without having regrets about what you did (or didn't) say.

One Important Perspective

We all want good relationships, right? You probably picked up this book for that reason, which likely means you're experiencing some challenges. You try to connect with others, but you hit different barriers with each person. Those barriers are real, and they feel big—and they keep us from connecting.

The lessons offered in this book don't involve changing others; they're all about taking responsibility for ourselves and our choices. Changing others is an exercise in futility. The things we'll discover will all be about things we have control over—which will always be personal. We can't fix anybody else; we can only work on ourselves.

That's the key to success. There are tons of things you don't have control of, and you'll be frustrated if you try to change those. In this journey, you'll only focus on yourself—how you think, how you respond, and the choices you make. You're a unique person, so you need a unique approach to connecting well with others. You won't have to change your personality or temperament; you'll simply become the best version of you that's possible.

That's where the magic happens. Ready to begin?

The Tale of Two Brains

No risk, no magic.

Anonymous

Our brains are pretty amazing.

There's a part of the brain (we'll call it "Brain One") where we make decisions, solve problems, and come up with creative ideas. When we have jobs, our companies are renting that portion of the brain. It's where we make intentional choices.

There's another part of the brain (we'll call it "Brain Two") that runs pretty much on autopilot. It's a wonderful part of the brain, because it helps us develop routines and habits that guide us through our lives.

Got a relationship problem you have to work out? Brain One goes into action. Want to improve your life? Call on Brain One. When we read self-help books or inspirational books that motivate us to grow and become more effective, it's Brain One that's impacted.

Brain One helps us change. It helps us dream. It helps us become better than we are.

Hooray for Brain One!

Brain Two isn't nearly as flashy. It runs quietly in the background, but it's critical to our survival.

When you want to try something new, Brain One shows up at your front door and says, "I'm in. Let's do this." What you're doing is new or different, so it takes intentional thought and effort. You have to focus, and Brain One is fully engaged.

The more we do it, the less effort it takes. It becomes routine. When that happens, Brain Two shows up and says, "OK, I'll take it from here." That's a good thing; imagine what it would be like if we never learned routines and had to constantly relearn everything.

Remember the day you drove to your current job for the first time? You had to use your GPS, study every turn, then figure out where to park and enter the building and how to find the correct office. Every step was intentional and took your whole focus. Now, you show up in your office and never think about how to get there. You just do it. In fact, most of us have days where we find ourselves in our office and can't remember how we got there. *That's Brain Two*. It helps us function before the coffee kicks in.

It takes between twenty-one and sixty-six days to develop a habit. Every habit starts in Brain One but eventually becomes the "new normal" in Brain Two.

Both parts are important, because they do different things. If I'm being chased by a hungry tiger, I don't want to use Brain One to make a list of my five best responses, prioritize them, and take action. *I just run*. Brain Two makes that happen.

Brain Two is also where our comfort zones are found, because they take a lot less effort than Brain One. At any age, we like our comfort zones. "Learning" takes effort; "having learned" doesn't. Without intentional effort to grow, we tend to stay in our comfort zones where we sit on the couch and eat chips.

The more we feel like we've figured out how life works and gained enough skills to get along, the more we settle in and get comfortable. We've learned enough of the basic skills to survive—but maybe not to thrive. We find routines that keep us in our comfort zones and follow those patterns day after day. They work for us and we stick with them. We eat meals at the same time, have the same types of conversations with our families, and watch the same shows every night.

We stay in Brain Two, living by default instead of design. The longer we stay there, the harder it is to get back to Brain One.

We weren't designed to live comfortable lives. We were designed to grow and change and make a difference.

Wilma was in her eighties when I was in my twenties. Everyone at church knew her for her energy and spunk. Whenever she saw me, she wanted to know if I was still growing.

"What are you reading right now?" she would ask, sneaking up behind me and slapping me on the shoulder. No matter what I answered, she would tell me the best book she had read recently, and why it was so good.

"You said you were going to get your doctorate," she would say. "Have you started? Why not?" Or maybe she would say, "Are you treating your wife well? So, what have you done for her lately?"

Wilma was growing. She was involved. She was living from Brain One.

Here's a simple question for you today: Are you living your life from the comfort of Brain Two or the vision of Brain One?

There's nothing wrong with Brain Two. We need that comfort zone as a place to rest and recover. It's the "home base" where we build the foundation for our life journey. It's where we rebuild our courage and strength.

It's our launching pad, not our landing pad.

Is It Time for a Brain Transplant?

If you've spent your whole life not having the courage to speak up when needed, it's tough to believe you can learn to do it.

The same thing is true if you consistently say the wrong thing at the wrong time and wonder why people react negatively. It feels like your communication patterns are part of who you are, not something you can change.

Instead of trying to improve, you've learned to adapt. You've found ways to handle the awkward situations where you don't know what to say or how to say it well, and you settle for disappointment. Maybe you've been told you need to "Say what's on your mind" or to be more outgoing. You're thinking, *Yeah, I'd love to. That's easy for you to say, but it's just not who I am.* It feels hard, and you'd have to become something you're not—so why even try?

That's the mindset that comes when Brain Two is running the show. Its job is to get you to do things routinely without thinking. It's filled with routines and habits, which is great. But it has no interest in doing anything differently.

When you've developed ways of coping, Brain Two says, "That's a good coping strategy. It's worked well for you. Let's keep doing it, OK?"

But you picked up this book because you aren't satisfied with coping and adapting. You want to change so you can communicate with more confidence. You've learned that it's possible— but is it worth the effort? You're at the fork in the road; one path (the one you're already on) is level and smooth, and Brain Two is your tour guide. The other path looks steep and rocky and filled with switchbacks, and Brain One is leading the way. Which way should you go?

Here are some things to consider:

- If you stay with Brain Two, you'll be OK—but nothing will change. You'll be using your current strategies in communication and will continue coping the way you have learned to in the past. You won't have to think about it; it will happen automatically.

- If you want to change, you'll have to choose Brain One. It might feel impossible and scary and overwhelming, but you won't be doing it alone. Brain One is an expert and knows the path well.
- With Brain One, you'll be stretched in new ways. But you won't have to do anything you're not capable of doing. You don't have to change your personality or your temperament; you get to be your own unique self (which is why it's even possible). You don't become something you're not; you become more of who you already are.
- The Brain One process doesn't require you to take giant leaps, only tiny steps. Tiny steps build on each other and eventually help you reach your goal.
- You won't stay on the Brain One path forever. Each step that becomes familiar builds a small skill that becomes comfortable. When that happens, it moves back to the Brain Two path, where it becomes your "new normal."

So, which brain is better? Both. The key is to be constantly moving between the two brains. We use Brain One to take a small step, to stretch and learn something new. It's like going to the hardware store and purchasing a new tool that we don't have. Once we've tried it out a few times and figured out how it works, we tuck it away in the toolbox of Brain Two so we can grab it whenever it's needed.

Tiny Steps Lead to Giant Outcomes

Whenever we fail at something big, it's painful. We instinctively think, *Well, that hurt. I'm not doing that ever again.* It's almost like that failure becomes a vaccination against growth. It's natural to avoid pain. But when we do, we also avoid progress and success.

The process of building our communication skills is often something people try by taking on too big of a change all at once. They think, *OK, I need to be more assertive. The next time I'm in a tough conversation, I'm going to force myself to say what I think and not worry about what anybody thinks.* That's a recipe for disaster and is usually painful enough that they don't try again for a really long time.

A better alternative is to take a single step—testing the waters in a safe conversation where you have an opinion that's different from the opinions of others. You don't have to make a big scene, just give a short, simple statement of your perspective. If you remain quiet, people think you agree with the majority.

If people are talking about what movie they want to attend and are leaning toward one you're not that interested in, you're probably used to going along with the crowd. Instead, just say, "You know, that's really not one I'm interested in. I'll go if that's what you all decide, just to be with you; it's just not very high on my list."

This might feel like a weak response because you gave in and went anyway. But at this stage, you're sticking your toes in the water of expressing your preferences. You've said something that was hard to say, and you survived. The next time you're in a similar situation, you'll find it easier to speak up again. When people are sharing ideas about a place to visit together, just make sure you express your suggestion so it's part of the mix. There's no guarantee where you'll end up, but you spoke up.

Soon you'll find that it's comfortable to express your thoughts in this way, and you'll realize you've moved that skill to the Brain Two path. With this foundation, you can move to the next step and repeat the process. There's no rush, because every step you take moves you forward.

I've always been amazed by airplane pilots. Flying is something I've wanted to learn my whole life because I've always been a huge fan of aviation. I've never done it, mostly because it seems so difficult. The consequences for making mistakes are a little unnerving. I've talked to pilots who fly daily, and they've done it so often it's completely routine. They're flying on the Brain Two path. Because they're so experienced and comfortable, they can instantly switch to Brain One when there's an emergency.

None of those pilots knew how to fly the first time they entered a cockpit. It's such a complicated process that they might have thought it would take forever to learn. It could have seemed overwhelming, and they could have given up. But they wanted it enough that they kept learning, one step at a time, honing their skills until they became natural.

The usual first step is to go on a demo flight with an instructor in a small plane. The instructor flies the plane while you watch and ask questions. I did that several times when I was much younger to get a sense of what it would be like to be at the controls. Once the plane was at flying altitude and level, the instructor let me take the controls briefly and showed me some very simple movements that would make slight changes to our flight. I wasn't flying the plane but got to try something that was so simple I thought, *Well, I could do this.* Years later, I still remember exactly what it felt like.

I never pursued flying, realizing it would take a lot of Brain One work before Brain Two would kick in. Because of that, I've missed out on something I probably would have loved.

That's exactly how growth works in any area: start with the tiniest steps, then practice them until they become routine.

The Journey Is Worth the Effort

Most people feel like their conversational style is just part of their wiring, as if it were embedded in their DNA. It seems permanent, and they feel like there's no hope of changing. You might be skeptical right now, unable to imagine ever feeling confident in every conversation.

Here's all you need to know: *effective conversation is a skill that can be learned.* As you experiment with each small step and gradually master it, your confidence will grow for the next step. You'll notice that each conversation becomes easier as you have more tools in your toolbox, and your confidence will increase.

Ready to step onto the path toward developing your skills of confident conversation? Let's start the journey together.

PART 1

The Case for Relevant Conversation

A few years ago I asked a trusted colleague for feedback. "I want to become a better person. What's one thing I could change to make that happen?" I asked.

His response: "You should get taller."

He was joking (I think). We both knew I had no control over my height, so I didn't give it much thought. The same applies to where I was born, who my parents were, my heritage, and what I did last week. Those things might bother me, but they're history. Trying to change them is futile.

There are, however, things I *can* change:

- Where I work.
- Where I live.
- Who I choose as friends.

- What I eat (and how much).
- What I read online.
- How much television I watch.
- What I say.

You might not believe you have control over those things because of long-standing patterns in your life. You know you should eat veggies to stay healthy, but you find yourself eating caramel sauce out of the jar with your fingers instead. You try to hold your tongue when someone frustrates you, but sarcasm oozes from you like a wet cat slipping out of your arms.

In which category does your communication fit? Maybe you've been hesitant in conversation for years, struggling to be confident in connecting with others. Your mind works better after a conversation than during it. Or maybe you feel invisible when you talk because nobody's listening. It's been happening for so long that you've come to believe the story you've crafted: *I'm not good at communicating and never will be.* So you give up, assuming you'll never be able to change. You believe you're in the "it's just the way I am" category.

But you picked up this book. That means you still have hope. Deep inside, you sense that change is possible. You think there are things you could do to become more confident in your communication skills.

The good news is that it's true. Effective communication is a skill that *anyone* can learn—regardless of your perceived limitations. You don't have to become a different person; you just have to learn new skills that fit who you are.

The better news is that it's not just about feeling confident or more compassionate in your conversations; it's about making a difference with your words. Conversation goes beyond exchanging words to using those words as powerful tools to impact others and society—to make a "dent" in the world.

There are plenty of books out there with tips and techniques for effective communication. I've written several of them.[1] But before we hone your techniques, we need to focus on what you want to accomplish—and why.

Why do you want to strengthen your communication skills?

What's your dream for changing your world?

How will things change for you if you become a better communicator?

Who will you impact?

What will happen if you *don't* take this journey to grow?

In this section, we'll discover why it's important to communicate with both confidence and compassion: confidence to speak up when it's needed, and compassion to choose your words carefully based on the needs of your listeners. We'll explore the kind of difference you're uniquely crafted to make and analyze the things that have been holding you back. Your unique temperament will be the foundation for success, since nobody else can do what you alone can accomplish. We'll also learn how caring deeply allows you to take the risk of confident confrontation.

When you discover your "why," you'll be ready to find out "how."

Ready for a change? Turn the page.

1

Making a Dent

If you think you're too small to make a difference,
you haven't spent a night with a mosquito.

African proverb

———

Do you ever feel invisible? Do you feel like you have more to
offer than people give you credit for?

You want to have influence with others, but nobody's
interested.

You say whatever you're thinking, but people get offended
or uncomfortable.

People listen politely when you talk, but nothing ever
happens.

You dream of changing the world, but you can't even influence the people around you.

It feels like you don't matter because your words never
seem to make a difference to others.

It's discouraging. It's depressing. You feel helpless and hopeless and start believing you have nothing to offer. Your self-esteem spirals downward, and it's hard to stay motivated. If nobody is listening, you believe you aren't worth listening to.

I'm writing this book during one of the most challenging times in recent history: the coronavirus pandemic paired with escalating racial tension. It's an interesting time, especially in terms of how people communicate. People who have never had a voice suddenly find themselves with the opportunity to express themselves in new ways, while those who have felt free to talk don't know what to say.

It's a new game for everyone. The rules of engagement are changing, and social media has become a hotbed of personal expression. People post their thoughts so they can be heard; others reply so they can be heard. Everybody wants to be heard, and they all get louder and stronger.

Everybody's talking, but it seems like nobody's listening. It's kind of like we're asking our kids to do something. If they don't respond, we get louder. When they still don't respond, our volume keeps going up, along with our emotions.

When I was scrolling through social media the other day, it occurred to me it could be a textbook on *ineffective* communication. If you want to learn how to make a difference in the world, you could probably study social media carefully—and then do the exact opposite.

Can you think of a time when you've read somebody's strongly worded post on social media and immediately changed your mind on a topic because of it? Probably not. That's what happens when talking increases and listening disappears. People want to make an impact but end up doing just the opposite. They replace substance with force or volume. They might get someone's attention by being loud, but that attention disappears when the listener realizes the person isn't saying anything of substance.

People might feel more passion about issues and express themselves on social media, but that doesn't mean their communication is effective. Their tendency to join the crowd makes them feel like they're "adding their voice," when it might actually be diluting their influence and impact. It's like spitting into Niagara Falls and wondering why nobody notices or cares.

So, how do you make a genuine impact when you're in conversation? *You need to gain weight.*

How Much Do You Weigh?

When I talk about gaining weight in this context, I'm not talking about adding a few pounds. I'm referring to increasing your contribution. The more you have to offer, the easier it is to get noticed.

That's why brain surgeons make more money than hospital interns. They're both extremely valuable, and both make significant contributions. But surgeons have paid the price in terms of education, time, and experience to provide results people will pay a fortune for.

Suppose you dropped a ping-pong ball from the top of a ten-story building, and it hit the lawn below. How much of a dent would it make? Not much. You wouldn't even be able to tell exactly where it hit.

Now suppose you dropped a bowling ball over the edge. Could you tell where it landed? Absolutely. It had greater weight, so it made more of an impact.

Let's look at this in a business context. You've been at your organization for a long time, but you get passed by for promotions. Other people are offered opportunities, but you're always overlooked. A lot of employees tell their boss, "I need a promotion and a raise." They figure that they've been there for a long time, so they should get paid more.

The manager looks at it differently. They're paying that employee for the value they bring in solving a business problem. Other than a simple cost-of-living raise, that manager won't be inclined to pay an employee more if they aren't getting more

35

value in return. If that employee takes the initiative to grow and increase their skills, provide creative solutions to problems, make a bigger contribution, and engage well, then there's good reason to pay them more.

The easiest way to get noticed at work is to increase the value you bring to the position. You become "weightier" in your work. When it comes to your contribution, assume that your manager is "paying by the pound" for the value you bring. Don't ask for a raise; grow bigger so you can make a greater impact.

This is also true in personal relationships—and just about every area of life. The louder you get, the less impact you'll have. The deeper you get, the more others will listen.

I deliver a keynote address called "How to Become a Thought Leader." It started when I noticed how many people write books or articles and refer to themselves as a "thought leader" in their personal information. It was harder to find someone who *didn't* describe themselves as a thought leader than someone who did.

Normally, we think of a thought leader as someone well-known who has original things to say. They usually have a perspective that's different from what most people are thinking, and their words cause other people to process things in new ways.

I decided to do a little informal research to see what someone could do if they wanted to become a true thought leader. I started by googling "How to become a thought leader." I found dozens of articles, blog posts, and white papers outlining the path to follow. Almost all of them were a variation on the same ideas, expressed in titles like "How You Can Become a Thought Leader in Thirty Days," or "Nine Simple Steps to Becoming a Thought Leader."

It sounded simple, so I read a number of those articles. They were filled with suggestions like these:

- Develop a clear strategy for social media.
- Show the mistakes people make and give solutions.

- Make your content interesting.
- Reply when people ask you questions online.
- Talk to experts to learn from them.
- Make presentations for experts so they'll notice you.
- Find curious audiences.
- Get really good at a niche topic.
- Organize your knowledge well, based on what your audience wants.
- Pitch yourself to the media.
- Post what others have said and add your comments.

Now, those aren't bad ideas in themselves. But in every resource I studied, there was one thing missing. It wasn't in a single article or resource I found but it's the one key to becoming a thought leader—and without it, nothing else works. It's vitally important but never urgent, so it's often overlooked.

What is it? What's the single most important thing you have to do to become a thought leader?

You have to think.

That's it. True thought leaders became thought leaders by having thoughts. Thoughts come from a serious commitment to thinking.

A thought leader without thoughts is like a shepherd without sheep. It's a nice title, but nobody will want their shepherding advice. They might have a great website and flashy marketing materials and celebrity endorsements. *But if shepherds don't smell like sheep, nobody's going to follow them.*

This is my favorite keynote to present because it's so simple but so revolutionary for people. In a society where everyone is trying to put themselves out there and get noticed, nobody wants to take the time and commitment needed to think deeply as a way of life. It's easier to put in earbuds and be constantly scrolling through the latest social media posts when we have a spare moment. But crafting time for deep thinking is where we get substance.

In other words, it's the best way to gain weight if you really want to add value to others and make a dent in the world.

Your Weight-Gaining Diet

I heard a nutritionist say it's important to include a lot of different colors on our plates because that provides the variety of nutrients our body needs. I assumed she was suggesting M&M's, but my wife let me know it was something different. (I was at least sharp enough to realize that if I regularly ate a plateful of M&M's instead of fish and veggies, I'd look a little different.) Our health is impacted by what we eat (as well as a number of other factors).

In the same way, our attitudes and beliefs come from what we put into our minds—the things we think about. Our thoughts come from our inputs: what we watch, what or who we listen to, and what we read. Those inputs are the ingredients from which we build our paradigms—the filters we use to evaluate life.

If we consistently fill our minds with the worst things in the news, surround ourselves with negative people, and read things that drag us down, we're going to feel negative about the world around us. We'll be fearful and anxious, victims of what others do or say. There's no way around it; we'll never have a stellar attitude or motivation to make a difference if the ingredients we take in are toxic. Our impact on others will slowly disappear like the vapor of a breath on a frosty morning.

That's why it's important to be intentional about what you take into your mind. What kind of a difference do you want to make? How do you want to impact others? Start with the outcomes you want, then determine what needs to be in your "diet."

If I want to bake a good cheesecake, I'll follow the recipe and use eggs, sugar, cream cheese, and other ingredients. But if I decide to add a handful of dirt, some leftover wall paint, and motor oil, nobody will want that cheesecake. Either way, the finished dessert will be a direct result of the ingredients I use.

The ability to influence others requires us to be intentional about what we pay attention to. Those ingredients directly determine the difference we make. It's also important to keep a large variety of ingredients in our mental cupboard. The greater the types of experiences we have, the greater the creativity we can have in shaping our perspectives.

About thirty years ago, I began traveling and teaching seminars in organizations ranging from Fortune 100 companies to mom-and-pop operations. I've interacted with different people on a daily basis inside those organizations, as well as with flight attendants, Uber drivers, restaurant personnel, and others along the way. When I was crafting speeches, writing books, and creating blog posts and articles during that time, I had a never-ending stream of ideas and real-life examples from which to draw.

Five years ago, I changed responsibilities in my job, traveling less and interacting with clients in more of a coaching role from my home office. I still talked to people, but I lost the richness that comes from face-to-face conversations. Over time, I started to run out of things to write about. I discovered that it's hard to write things that make an impact when I'm just sitting on my couch making things up out of my head.

Last year, I started traveling to meet with clients in-person again through speaking opportunities as well as coaching relationships and strategy sessions—and the inspiration came back. The richer the experiences I had and the more varied the conversations, the more ingredients I had available to build from. Now I'm able to write more consistently with fresher ideas, and more people are feeling the impact. You could say I've gained a little weight.

Stocking Our Cupboards

I've found three specific ingredients that work together to increase our weight in this context: *time*, *intention*, and *resilience*. Let's break each of these down.

Time

When our kids learned how to drive, we wanted them to have their first accidents as soon as possible (minor, with nobody getting hurt). They were actually good drivers, and they knew the rules of the road. But soon enough, those accidents happened.

My daughter rear-ended someone on the freeway when he stopped quickly, and she knocked his bumper off. My son ran into the car ahead of him when he got distracted by a pretty girl driving the car next to him.

They weren't experienced. They didn't have "street smarts" yet. These first accidents made them better drivers. As we all discover, it takes years of driving to really hone our driving instincts.

Likewise, trying to build a life of impact doesn't happen overnight; it takes time. "Weight" comes through a collection of life experiences over time—growing through the tough stuff.

I once heard a speaker say, "Never expect anything of value out of a person until they're thirty-five." I don't completely agree, and it's probably different for everyone. But I do remember thirty-five was a tipping point for me. Before that, I felt like I was contributing, but I was still in my growing and learning stage. Shortly after I turned thirty-five, I realized I could start making a serious contribution to others in a whole new way. For the first time, my conversations started making a difference for others.

A baby impacts people because they're cute. A twenty-year-old impacts people because of who they're becoming. People can't jump from two to twenty; they have to grow one year at a time.

There are no shortcuts to developing the skills of influence through our words. A diamond isn't formed overnight, and neither is a life. If we try to short-circuit the process, it becomes a get-mature-quick scheme. High-quality results don't come from quick solutions.

Intention

Author and speaker John Maxwell wrote a book called *Failing Forward*.[1] It's based on the premise that we grow the most through our mistakes. If we avoid mistakes, we avoid growth. The goal, then, is to fail as often as possible. That means we're being intentional about growing.

My friend Dave had been setting big goals but hesitated to pursue them for fear of failure. He and I attended a conference together last year where a speaker talked about how grateful he was for his failures. Today, Dave said he has a new goal: "I want to fail at four big things this year."

That's being intentional. "Gaining weight" doesn't happen by accident. It happens by making choices and taking risks to get better in our lives.

Resilience

Resilience can be defined as the ability to successfully cope with a crisis and "return to pre-crisis status quickly."[2] This ties in directly with failure. It doesn't mean it doesn't hurt to get knocked down; it just means we get back up again quickly. It's a pattern that has to be learned over time as we intentionally choose not to get stuck in our mistakes and failures. We learn from them, grow a bit, and move forward.

Life isn't easy. We all face challenges daily. Many people become hardened and cynical, feeling they've been dealt a bad hand.

But since you're reading this book, I know you're different. You're probably facing similar challenges, but you're trying to turn them into stepping-stones. When people see you handling the same challenges they have but responding differently, they'll take notice. Who you are becomes a beacon to help them think and act in new and effective ways.

Steps for Gaining Weight

Do you want your communication to become an easy, natural process when you're interacting with others? Try these simple steps to hone your conversational skills:

- Just for today, don't worry about making a huge impact with your words. Pick one simple thing you could do today for someone else that would make their life richer. Use your words to make a difference right where you are, with whatever you've got and whoever you're with.
- Take a small risk today. Pick one thing that you're not sure will be successful and do it anyway. Risk failure. If it happens, celebrate—you've grown.
- When something goes wrong today, don't get stuck there. Acknowledge it and move forward.

If you feel like people are ignoring you, don't wait for them to change; become a different person yourself. Gain some "weight," and you'll catch their attention!

2

What's Holding You Back?

It is more powerful to speak up than to silently resent.

Anonymous

The white minivan drifted into my lane just as I was about to pass it. I braked to avoid a collision just before the driver jerked back to the other lane. The van was moving way under freeway speed and gradually drifting back and forth—first to the left lane, then the right. After watching for a few minutes, the word *impaired* surfaced in my mind.

I had a choice. I knew I should call 911 to report them before they caused an accident. But then a ton of excuses ran through my mind.

I'm too far away to have their license number.
I'm not sure what kind of car it is.
The police won't be able to find the car while it's moving.
I might be wrong, and the person is just distracted.
I don't want to use my phone while I'm driving.

I'm sure somebody else will call.

I don't want to get involved.

You might be thinking, *Of course you would call. It could be a tragedy, and it's only common sense to report it. There's too much at stake.* You can't imagine anyone *not* calling.

Or you might be thinking, *Yep—that's me. I wish I had the courage to speak up, but I know I'd just leave it to someone else.*

What would you do?

We've all been in situations where we felt the need to speak up but just couldn't make it happen:

- A toddler is kicking the back of your seat repeatedly on a long flight. You're irritated but don't want to cause a scene when everyone around would be listening—so you suffer in silence.

- Three teenagers are talking in the dark theater about three rows ahead of you as the movie begins. Ten minutes later, they haven't let up. You don't want to come across as a grumpy person, so you move to the other side of the theater and hope somebody else will jump in.

- The service is slow, the waiter is unfriendly, and the food isn't cooked correctly. You don't want to be a complainer, so you don't say anything. You just leave and then post a negative review online.

- An extended family member becomes inappropriate during a holiday gathering, and you want to say something. In the past, you've tried to speak up—but your words just didn't come together well and you appeared scattered and emotional.

In all of those situations, there's a common thread: how other people will respond. Our responses are influenced by what others will think, so we simmer in silence. Every time it happens, we think, *What's wrong with me? I wish I could speak up when I need to instead of clamming up.* There's a low-grade guilt that rises, and it's one we've experienced many times over the years.

Don't we all have mixed emotions in those kinds of situations? Have you experienced times when you really wanted to speak up but were afraid of coming across as insensitive? Have you blurted something out in an emotional conversation that you wished you could take back? It happens to all of us, because we're human. We're not perfect.

Or you might be someone who uses aggressiveness to get people to respond to you. You've had times when nobody was listening, and you learned that being tough gets their attention. You know from their reactions that you're alienating them. But hey, it gets the job done, right? People do what you want, but you're lacking deep relationships. It might not happen all the time, but it bubbles to the surface when you're frustrated—and you regret it later. How can you learn to share your thoughts with confidence in a way that shows compassion and strengthens relationships?

We'll cover assertiveness in a different chapter—how to speak your mind in a way that actually advances the conversation rather than stopping it. For now, let's explore the things that keep us from expressing what we need to say. What prevents us from contributing when something really needs to be said?

The Reasons for Reticence

I was literally the last one picked for a kickball game in fifth grade. The "captains" of each team took turns calling out the names of the people they wanted on their team, gradually narrowing down the group of potential players until everyone had been picked—except me.

That was bad enough. But then both sides tried to give me to the other team. "You can have him," one side said. "No, that's OK. You take him." I don't remember what happened during the game, but I doubt I was considering a career in major league sports.

Nobody likes rejection. In fact, avoiding it seems to be hardwired into our brains. One study showed that rejection follows the same pathways in our brains as physical pain.[1] It's one of the reasons that rejection "hurts" as much as physical pain—and if we take an over-the-counter painkiller, we'll actually feel better in both instances.

Have you ever decorated a room, made a presentation to a group, or cooked a meal for others? Twenty people told you how much they liked it, and one person criticized you. Which feedback did you remember the longest? That's right, it's the negative response. It doesn't make sense, but our minds bypass the positive and zero in on the negative. Somehow, negative things feel worse than positive things feel better.

You go on vacation to a tropical location and have an amazing time. Each morning you relax on the hotel balcony overlooking the ocean while sipping your coffee or tea, and you go on excursions during the day that are interesting and energizing. You forget about the pressures of work and everyday living and manage to clear your head for some much-needed restoration.

Then one night at 3:00 a.m., someone pulls the fire alarm and the hotel has to be evacuated. You throw on a robe and dash down the stairs to assemble with other guests on the lawn while the fire department goes through the building to make sure it's safe. Two hours later you're allowed back into your room.

When you get home, which story do you tell people: relaxing on the balcony or having to evacuate? Usually, it's the drama that sticks in our minds—the negative events that stand out from the background of serenity.

That's what happens with rejection. We have vivid memories of the times we've been hurt by the words or actions of others, so we subconsciously do everything we can to avoid getting hurt in the present or in the future. Our experience tells us that the things we say can lead to pain, so we avoid speaking our minds (or we blurt things out in frustration and regret it later).

Here are some of the reasons we're afraid to communicate:

- *We're afraid of people rejecting us.* We believe that if someone doesn't like what we say, we might assume they don't agree with us and think we're stupid or irrelevant. It's not worth risking that possibility, so we just keep quiet.

- *We're afraid of people's emotions.* If it's someone we've seen lash out at others in the past, we'll avoid stirring things up so they won't lash out at us. We're uncomfortable with anger or intimidation and don't know how to respond, so we make sure there's no reason for it to happen.

- *We don't have confidence we can effectively express what we're thinking.* We feel like we could present our opinions if we had time to carefully craft our ideas, but that rarely happens during the conversation. We think of all the best things to say after they're gone. (This could be an introvert thing, where we need time to process before sharing.)

- *We're people pleasers.* We've developed a lifelong pattern of finding our personal worth in the reactions of others. That means we have to craft every interaction to make people like us, because our self-worth is at stake. We've learned to avoid anything that would cause others to think negatively toward us.

- *We're in a public setting and feel like everyone is listening and critiquing us.* It's bad enough to risk rejection in a one-on-one conversation. But when it happens in a group setting, we're not just risking that person's rejection; that negative perspective could infect the whole group and multiply the impact.

There's a common thread between all of these issues: we want people to accept us and treat us well. It hurts when they don't, so we'll do whatever is needed to make sure they feel positively about us.

How to Get People to Treat You Well

It's common to believe that the other person is the problem. If they're not treating us the way we want them to, we scramble for solutions to get them to change. Maybe we decide not to speak up when we want to so they won't have anything to criticize. Maybe we say yes when we really want to say no. Maybe we try to show them the error of their ways so they'll act differently. In any case, we want them to change.

What's that called? *Futility.* It's hard enough to change ourselves; what makes us think we'll be able to change others? That's discouraging, because it feels like we'll always be stuck as a victim of their words and actions.

Fortunately, there's a simple way of dealing with people that increases the likelihood of them treating you well. It's based on the Golden Rule: do unto others as you would have them do unto you. We'll go into more detail as we move forward. For now, we'll divide it into two basic categories:

1. How we treat others.
2. How we respond to the way others treat us.

Let's explore both to see how they apply.

How We Treat Others

We teach other people how to treat us by the way we treat them. They might have gotten into a pattern of how they relate to people in general, but that doesn't mean it's the only option. Regardless, there's no guarantee of how they'll respond, and we'll be frustrated if that's how we measure success. We can't control how others treat us, but we can *influence* it by the way we treat them:

- When we treat people with respect, there's a much better chance that they'll treat us with respect.
- When we ignore them, they'll tend to ignore us.
- When we constantly express frustration with them, they'll probably get frustrated with us.
- When we show them kindness, they might learn to do the same.
- When we give them our full attention, they'll see an example that they might follow.

Most people won't even recognize what's happening, but when they see a behavior demonstrated, it gives them a template to try it out themselves.

Remember, we can't change them; we can only change ourselves. This means becoming the kind of person who treats others well. We're not doing it to manipulate them; we're being ourselves. In other words, we're living with *integrity*—not trying to pretend to be something we're not.

How We Respond to the Way Others Treat Us

Jerilynn started her job four months ago. From the first moment, her boss would drop by with something he needed her to do "right away." Everything had a sense of urgency connected to it, and she was getting overwhelmed. She was grateful for the job and wanted to make a good impression, so she didn't feel she could push back or say no. No matter how hard she worked, she couldn't get ahead. She would eat lunch at her desk each day just to try to catch up.

Lynne, in the next cubicle, never seemed rushed. She took breaks as needed, left the office on time, and showed up relaxed each morning. At first, Jerilynn felt like Lynne was getting special treatment because she didn't work as hard.

One day, she overheard Lynne's conversation with their boss when he dropped by. "I need this before lunch," he said. "It's really important."

Lynne's response surprised Jerilynn. "Well, of course, I'd be happy to do that. Not a problem at all. I do need your help, though. You've asked me to work on these other three things this morning, and they'll take the entire morning to finish. I'm happy to do this new one if you'd like, but one of these other ones won't get done until later. Which one would you like me to postpone?"

Lynne didn't say no to her boss but didn't just accept every assignment exactly as it was given. She treated him with respect by acknowledging his role, then asked for his partnership around each task. He in turn respected her challenge and helped her triage the other tasks, and he gradually began to prioritize assignments before giving them to her. That open communication and mutual respect became the framework for their working relationship.

People learn how to treat us based on what we accept from them. Treating them the way we would like to be treated moves us from being a victim to building a realistic relationship. The way we respond either reinforces or decreases the likelihood of them continuing their behavior.

Does it always work? Of course not. Some people have spent years in patterns of ineffective communication, and nothing we do appears to make a difference. It seems like they'll never change, no matter what we do.

That's the point. The solution will never come from trying to force someone to change. Our best hope is to change how we treat others and how we respond to the way they treat us. We'll be looking at more specific ideas throughout the rest of this book. But they're all based on things *we* can do, instead of expecting others to change.

Figure out what you can and can't control. When you focus on the things you can control (yourself, your attitude, and your choices), you have a credible claim to peace and sanity. When you focus on things you can't control (everything else), you let others determine how you feel.

Practicing the Golden Rule

It doesn't take years to change the way we treat others. It just takes two simple steps:

1. Consider how you want to be treated.
2. Treat others that way.

As you go through today, be aware of the conversations you have with others. In each one, ask yourself, *How would I like this person to treat me?* Then find a way to treat them that way.

- If you would like a cashier to treat you like a real person, smile at them and thank them for what they do.
- If you want someone at a social event to initiate a conversation with you, initiate one with them first.
- If you want to become friends with a coworker, reach out and ask about the ups and downs of their job.

51

- If you want your teenager to listen to you, listen to them first without trying to fix anything.

Start small, and don't worry about how the other person responds. Just reach out with integrity, treat them the way you want to be treated, and then watch what happens.

It could change everything—or it might just change you. But isn't that a good place to start?

3

Your Temperament Is Your Superpower

Never attempt to teach a pig to sing.
It wastes your time and annoys the pig.

Robert Heinlein

It's 5:15 a.m. It's dark outside, and peaceful. I have a two-hour drive to get to an early morning meeting with a client, so I decide to grab a cup of coffee for the trip.

I pull the door open at a local coffee shop. I'm barely inside when I hear shouting from across the room: "Good morning, sir! Great to see you so early in the morning. My, you're an early riser. How's your day going?"

Now, I'm a morning person. I'm up early every day, and I always look forward to the quiet of the predawn hours. But the key word is *quiet*. There's nothing better than starting my day slowly, savoring the silence before the world starts to speak. It fills my emotional tank so I have fuel for the day.

Hearing a loud, high-energy greeting from a boisterous barista was like having the smoke alarm go off in the bedroom in the middle of the night. He had my attention, but I was ready to turn around and walk back outside.

He was on a mission to energize others, dealing caffeine to jump-start their day. I'm sure he meant well and was probably hired for his energy and enthusiasm. But he made me tired.

Do you have an early bird in your life who tends to be just a little too . . . well, *happy*? Some people just feel good in the morning and are noisier than others, but they're genetically wired to start their day with their emotional pedal to the metal. They're excited about the early hours and want to share it with the world.

A much larger group love mornings but do so quietly. As the morning progresses, they start engaging more and often do their best work before lunch. That time is their "sweet spot." They're usually at their conversational best early in the day. At night, they might have trouble stringing coherent thoughts together and forming multisyllabic words. They try, but they're out of fuel.[1]

What about night people? Night people have an entirely different perspective on the world. They look at morning people and wonder what's wrong with them. They feel like morning people are missing the best part of the day, the late-night hours, and can't imagine what it would be like to get up at sunrise (or why anyone would want to).

My son, Tim, is a night person. When he was little, he would sleep in until we woke him and would fight his early bedtime every night. He absolutely *loved* nighttime—the later, the better. I had always imagined getting up with my son to watch the sunrise or go on a hike, so it was pretty disappointing to learn he didn't share my enthusiasm. He's naturally at his best as evening approaches, and it's his favorite time of day. It's tougher for him now, because he manages a chain of restaurants and often has to be at work by 5:00 or 6:00 a.m. to open. He's gotten used to it, but his basic wiring is nocturnal.

We took a family vacation to Hawaii when our kids were in their early teens. My morning-person daughter, Sara, and I would get up and grab some coffee or juice to take to the beach, where we would sit and watch the sunrise. Tim wanted to sleep in. When we would wake him up, he was pretty grumpy. We'd go for an early breakfast, but he wouldn't talk. He barely ate his food, slumped over his meal, and disengaged from conversation.

I thought it was because he was a teenager. I was concerned about his attitude and felt like he was just being rude and rebellious. I was worried about our relationship. I tried to connect, but nothing happened.

I tried to "fix" him. It didn't work.

He was perceptive enough to discern what was happening. One morning, he mustered up enough energy to form a few words. He put his head up, looked me in the eye, and said, "Just give me two hours. Don't talk to me for two hours. We'll be fine." And we were.

Put a morning person at a breakfast table with a night person, and you'll watch a conversational sideshow. The morning person is energized, curious, and engaged, while the night person has trouble keeping up. In the evening, the same scenario is repeated—but in reverse.

Hardwired for Life

I learned a lot about communication from Tim that day.

I knew how I saw the world and assumed that if others could adopt that perspective, they would enjoy it just as much as I did. Deep inside, I was trying to get everybody to view life the way I did. *If they just knew what they were missing*, I thought, *obviously they would want to change. That would make both of us happier.*

I felt like it was my job to change others. But they didn't need changing.

Sure, there are areas where all of us can get better. We can grow and stretch, overcome habits, and challenge the way we think. But our basic temperament is our "hardwiring," and it's something we were born with. Trying to change that wiring is like trying to turn a tree into an elephant. It's obvious that it's impossible, and we wouldn't try. Yet we assume it's possible with other people.

We can change our choices, but not our DNA. If our happiness depends on other people becoming more like us, we're going to be frustrated for a long time. This goes the other way too. If we think we need to become like others to be fulfilled, happiness will always be out of reach.

Consider how introverts and extroverts feel about conversation. Introverts often wish they could be as outgoing and quick with words as extroverts, feeling like they're "not enough" the way they are. They automatically think, *What's wrong with me?* Extroverts tend to think quickly and speak quickly, and may speak up without realizing they've said something insulting or awkward. They often can't understand why introverts don't just speak up more. They think, *What's wrong with them?*

Introverts aren't necessarily shy (that's a different issue), but they tend to be internal processors. They hear information but need time to think through it before responding. Extroverts are external processors. They form their thoughts by talking to others, so they're often seen as confident.

Introverts think deeper while extroverts think faster. An introvert can be in a conversation with an extrovert about a topic and might feel frustrated that they can never think of the best response in the moment. Their response comes, but not until later.

So, which is best—introversion or extroversion? Or night people versus morning people? Or any other area where people are naturally different?

The best is *whichever one we're naturally wired to be.* We get in trouble when we compare, wishing we were more like someone else. If our temperament is our hardwiring, it's futile to wish it were different. Wishing we were something we're not ensures we'll be frustrated and unable to influence anyone—or become confident in our conversations.

The key is to recognize what we can change and what we can't. It's a two-step process.

1. Figure out what we *can't* change—then accept and capitalize on who we are.
2. Figure out what we *can* change—and begin the journey of growth.

Your temperament is your superpower for life. Instead of wishing for someone else's temperament, you thrive exponentially when you fully accept your own wiring and build on it. As pastor and author John Ortberg says, you become "youier."[2] He suggests that it's like taking an old piece of furniture and refinishing it. You're not rebuilding it into something different but making it the absolute best version of itself it can possibly be.

We need to become students of ourselves and become "you-ier."

There's another upside to building on our natural wiring: we can relax. It takes a lot of energy to try to change who we were created to be, because it'll never happen. Once we catch the vision for who we are and what we can become, all of our energy goes into growing. We're doing what's possible, not what's impossible—and that's freeing.

How Temperament Impacts Communication

Typically, introverts struggle with *courage* in conversation, while extroverts struggle with *compassion*. Every person is different, of course. But introverts can feel intimidated and hold back from saying what they really want and need to say. Extroverts are usually comfortable expressing their thoughts but don't always consider how those words are impacting the people around them.

It's like night and morning people. My wife and I meet with two other couples about once a month, rotating homes for meeting. We're good friends, and usually are reading a book together as an excuse to connect. We start with dinner around 6:00 p.m., then talk about what we've read until about 9:00. It's always great to share ideas and talk through the applications to our daily lives.

Unfortunately, most of them are night people, while I start losing the ability to form coherent words around 8:00. I'm still engaged and listening, but I'm out of fuel for the day. I used to feel bad about not contributing at that point, especially when the most outgoing friend would say, "Mike, you haven't said much. What's your take on this?" I always felt like saying, "Ask me tomorrow morning and I'll let you know." Over time, we've learned how each other are wired, and we're OK with letting each other be who we are. (A couple of times we've gotten together early in the morning, and it's great to see the roles reverse.)

No matter what our temperament, we can learn to communicate with confidence *and* compassion. It's never easy for me to have a courageous conversation, but it's easier first thing in the morning than late at night. But if that conversation needs to happen with a night person, I'll shoot for mid-to-late afternoon when both of us have a chance.

How can we learn to let others be exactly who they are? Here are three perspectives to consider.

First, we can recognize they're not "wrong," just different from us. Someone said, "If two people are exactly alike, one of them is unnecessary." There's no need to turn into someone else—that identity is reserved for them.

Second, we don't try to "fix" them. A friend of mine (a night person) said, "If people were meant to pop out of bed in the morning, they would sleep in toasters." We might not be able to change someone else, but we can choose how we respond to them. If we get irritated with them, it can ruin our whole day—and we've given them control over our emotions. It's better to simply observe but not internalize their actions. As the Beatles sang, "Let it be."[3]

Third, we can be honest, but kind. When someone has more energy than we're ready for in the morning or evening, it's easy to let frustration build. We feel like saying, "Will you just chill? You're driving me crazy!" (But that probably wouldn't be edifying.) Instead, choose an honest response, and say it graciously.

I once watched a night person converse with an extra-chatty person in the early morning (like my barista). At one point he put up his hand like a stop sign, as if to say, "Hold on." Then he continued, "Hey, I gotta tell you—you're a great conversationalist in the morning, but I'm not. I need you to slow down a little. My thoughts don't connect very well this early. But if you want to wait until tonight, I'm all in."

Your Lenses Are Your Own, Nobody Else's

All of us have glasses through which we see and interpret the world. Those glasses are a combination of two things: our basic temperament we were born with, and the experiences we've lived through over the years. Those glasses determine how clearly we see things. We don't stop to think about the lenses; we just assume that what we're seeing is accurate.

If you and I disagree but I'm convinced I'm right, I feel like I just need to share my position more clearly. You're doing the same thing. Why? We have different lenses that make us see the same thing differently. If we're both trying to convince each other our position is right, we're just fogging up our lenses.

Our history, background, culture, experiences, and perspectives filter what we see and form the lenses we look through. Clarity is important in communication, but it's not the only thing needed.

The first step in becoming a world-class communicator is to recognize that *you are not me*. Instead of trying to change you, I begin by encouraging you to show me what you see through your glasses. When I start a conversation that way, it encourages you to do the same. When we both look through each other's lenses, it builds trust.

How do we do that? It's called *listening*.

When we see conversation in that way, it's no longer a matter of who's right and who's wrong. We acknowledge we're different people. Communication breaks down when we try to make others see things our way. There's definitely a place for clearly expressing our thoughts, but it comes later in the conversation—not at the beginning. That allows us to explore and accept the unique thoughts of each person instead of critiquing them. Conversation becomes a tool for learning and understanding, for courage and compassion. Listening lubricates the conversation so real connection can happen.

The End of the Story

Several years after my conversation with my son in Hawaii, he gave me an unusual gift for Father's Day. He made me a certificate that said he would take me to a midnight movie. I said, "Hey! I thought you were supposed to give gifts that people actually want! A midnight movie? You know I'll fall asleep!"

"Take a nap," he said. "You'll be fine."

I wasn't really looking forward to it, but he really wanted me to go. So I took a nap.

It was an action movie, so I was able to stay awake through the whole thing. We walked out of the theater about 2:15 a.m.

There weren't very many other people at the theater, so we stood on the street by ourselves.

It was quiet. It was peaceful. It was *amazing*. I had the same feeling I do when I get up at dawn.

He stood quietly for a moment, staring off into the dark quietness as if to just take it all in.

"This is my world," he said. "I wanted you to see it with me."

I saw it. I felt it. And I loved him for sharing it with me.

That's how world-class communication begins: giving up our own agenda and entering another person's world.

4

Confrontation, Not Conflict

Make sure everybody in the boat is rowing
and not drilling holes when you're not looking.

Anonymous

———

Yesterday, I watched a video clip of a famous reporter known
for her confrontational style. She was interviewing an expert
she strongly disagreed with and was working to shoot holes in
his position through logic and debate. He was confident in his
position and never seemed intimidated by her approach. He
came across as level-headed and respectful, while she appeared
angry and forceful—interrupting and attacking with rapid-fire
accusations to throw him off-balance.

He didn't budge. When he wasn't intimidated and responded
with precision instead of malice, it became obvious that the
reporter was using a well-developed confrontation approach
she employed to "win" arguments. She wasn't an expert in the
topics she was discussing as much as she excelled in her technique. Over years of interviews, she had developed a way of
making people stumble in their words or presentation so they

would appear inept and uncertain. This time, her skill wasn't enough to keep her on top of the debate.

We've all watched those types of interviews with a mix of pain and pleasure, depending on which side we're on. If we're on the side of the reporter, we love seeing them embarrass their subject. If we're on the side of the person being interviewed, we cringe when they stumble and cheer when they hold their own. Some people are comfortable sparring with someone in that situation, but most of us think, *I'd never be able to stand up against someone like that.* Even if we know our position well, we're afraid of someone twisting the facts to make us look foolish and of not knowing how to respond.

That's one of the biggest reasons we avoid confrontation in our relationships. We're afraid that if we confront a spouse, teenager, friend, or coworker with an issue, it will turn into a heated conversation that feels intimidating, and we won't know how to respond. We feel like we're bringing a water pistol to a gunfight. Who in their right mind would choose confrontation when they could simply stay quiet and avoid stirring up tough conversations?

Someone who wants to develop world-class relationships.

The Power of Caring Confrontation

We have to redefine the word *confrontation.*

If we can move confrontation out of the category of heated debate and see the value of the process, we might see it as a priceless addition to our conversational toolkit.

Confrontation is like a power tool. Power tools can be used to accomplish great things, but when used improperly they can create great damage. That's why manuals for power tools always begin with multiple pages of safety instructions that include terms like "bodily harm" and "death" if we use the tool carelessly. We purchase the tool for what it can do but recognize the importance of learning to use it correctly and wearing appropriate protective gear when doing so.

I looked up the word *confront* in the dictionary and saw this definition: "To meet someone face-to-face with hostile or argumentative intent."[1] It reminded me of what happens when an intruder breaks into your house in the darkness, and you have to take action to protect your family and possessions. It's terrifying, and you don't want to do it. But the consequences of hiding in the darkness are greater than taking the risk. You confront because you have to.

If we only see confrontation as hostile or argumentative, we'll avoid it as something negative and painful. We'll assume that bringing up a tough issue with someone will always be a horrible experience. We're wired to avoid pain, so we'll ignore it and hope things will get better over time.

Then I kept reading and found a second meaning for *confront*: "To face up to or deal with a problem or difficult situation." That perspective completes the definition. Without recognizing that aspect of confrontation, we'll see every encounter as a tough media interview rather than a way to grow and strengthen our relationships. When we don't deal with serious issues, they grow under the surface—only to reappear in the future, seemingly bigger than before.

It's like avoiding a physical exam because you're afraid of what the doctor might find. Maybe you've been having symptoms similar to something your parents had before a hard diagnosis, and you know the painful treatment they had to go through. If we focus only on the pain, we'll avoid dealing with the issue. If we focus on the healing, we're more willing to get help. The surgeon "confronts" the issue—not because they want to hurt you, but because they can remove the dangerous condition.

In relationships, we tend to avoid confrontation for a number of reasons.

1. **We're afraid of rejection.** What if they get angry or reject us, and it damages the relationship irreparably? We feel like it's not worth the risk.

2. **We've had negative confrontations in the past.** We've felt the pain of those encounters, and we don't want to feel that pain again.

3. **We don't want to hurt the other person's feelings.** We care deeply about them, and it makes us uncomfortable to see them in pain—especially if we're the one causing it.

4. **It's not that big of a thing.** Sure, they're frustrating us or doing something we wish they wouldn't. But it's not that important, so why bother stirring things up?

5. **We're not completely clear on our perspective.** We know we're frustrated, and the issue is big enough that it needs to be dealt with. We just haven't thought it through enough to be completely clear on what we're thinking. We don't want to enter a discussion until we feel confident about our side.

Some people avoid confrontation because they're afraid it means they have to become an irritating person no one likes. It's critical to have the right mindset about how to use this tool of confrontation safely, and what circumstances warrant it. The goal isn't to become an obnoxious person; it's to develop the skill of confrontation in order to use it effectively in situations where no other tool will work as well.

It's also not a tool to use with every person we disagree with or who rubs us the wrong way. We need to be selective about who we confront, and it will generally be the people we have a vested interest in (or someone whose words or actions are impacting those people). This will include

   people we deeply care about, including the friends we do life with;

people we're closely related to, such as spouses and family members; and

people we're responsible for, such as our children or employees.

In this book, we're not developing debating skills or learning to argue for the purpose of sparring over opinions. We're focusing on everyday encounters with people who are in our lives and deserve our best efforts. The goal is to make our relationships stronger, not to become skilled in dismantling the arguments of others so we "win" the debate.

Confrontation should be like surgery. It's never the first treatment option, and it isn't used for minor issues. It's for when lesser solutions just won't bring healing, and the issue is too important to ignore.

Mindset: The Foundation for Powerful Confrontation

Confrontation has value when it's used in the right circumstances, for the right reasons, and in the right way. (In future chapters we'll talk about the details of the process so you can practice with precision, confronting with both courage and grace.) Learning to confront well starts with you, not the other person. It means you're thinking clearly about your own perspective before attempting to influence others. What happens in your head comes before dealing with what's happening in someone else's head.

There are three areas to consider when developing the proper mindset:

1. Checking your motives.
2. Acting early.
3. Building trust.

Checking Your Motives

There are a lot of reasons you might need to confront someone. Maybe you've seen the impact their choices are having on themselves and others, and you realize something needs to be done. When you've reached that place and have strong emotions about the situation, it's easy to become blinded to your true motives. Emotion and logic don't often play well together; the stronger the emotion, the tougher it is to be objective about what's really happening.

Here are some questions to ask yourself to make sure your mindset is in the right place:

- Am I the best person to confront them?
- What do I really want to see happen as a result?
- Do I have underlying emotions I might be ignoring, such as anger or hurt that's clouding my judgment?
- Inside, do I want them to feel punished and suffer the consequences of what they're doing?
- Have I been talking to others about them to rally support for my position?
- Am I convinced I'm right and they're wrong?
- Can I listen to try to understand their perspective before presenting mine?
- Am I open to changing my perspective after hearing what they have to say?
- How will I feel if nothing changes?

Simply stated, take time to analyze your own motives and feelings before confronting anyone. Being scrupulously honest about your own motives can ensure your approach is intentional and caring. You'll feel more confident because you're having a genuine conversation instead of unconsciously manipulating the encounter.

Acting Early

The best time to take action with any uncomfortable situation is when it first appears. It's natural to try to wait it out, hoping it'll get better. But like a single cancer cell, it rarely stays dormant once it's in a body. The longer we wait, the worse it can get.

The other day I read about a rancher in a Midwestern rural community who has hundreds of cows. His cows roam freely over miles of pastureland, and they seem to lead pretty comfortable lives.

At certain times of the year, cloudbursts come through those pastures on a regular basis. The storms are pretty severe and move pretty slowly—and they only last about five minutes. The cows don't like those mini-storms, so they instinctively try to run away from them.

The problem is that cows don't run very fast. In fact, they run about the same speed as the storms are moving. So the cows run along with the storm, and they get soaked a lot longer. If they just stayed in one place and faced the storm, sure, it would be uncomfortable. But it would be over a lot faster. By running with the storm, they prolong the pain.[2]

Relationships are like that. When something feels uncomfortable and needs to be addressed, we don't look forward to it. We put off talking about it. We procrastinate. We hope it'll get better. The longer we put it off, the more the issue grows and the worse it becomes. By putting off the tough conversation, we prolong the discomfort. We run with the storm.

Even if it's uncomfortable, we need to start dealing with tough issues as soon as they surface. If we wait, it tends to get worse, and the issues start growing.

Develop the mindset that you're willing to have a tough conversation as soon as an issue appears. If you address the issue early, you'll be able to do it without the frustration that builds over time, and it will be a caring confrontation. The longer you wait, the tougher the conversation will be. Tough conversations take time, but *not having* tough conversations takes longer.

Building Trust

The pilot's voice comes over the intercom: "Ladies and gentlemen, this is your captain. I have an announcement, and there's good news and bad news. The bad news is that if you look out the right side of the cabin, you'll notice one of the engines is on fire. If you look out the left side, another engine is on fire. We've also lost our radar and communication with the ground, and we're almost out of fuel."

He continues: "The good news is that we're making really good time."

Have you ever worked for someone who put a positive spin on the current situation, no matter how bad it was? They're probably doing so because they want to encourage their people, and figure that bad news will discourage them. The effect is usually the opposite. You know things are worse than they're saying, so you're convinced they're hiding the truth. When that happens, trust is broken. When there's no trust, the foundation of the relationship has eroded.

This happens in marriages when one spouse handles the finances this way. The other spouse says, "Do we have enough money to buy this? It's on sale." The first spouse doesn't want to disappoint them, so they say, "Sure. Go ahead." But when it happens repeatedly, it soon becomes obvious that the accounts are overdrawn—and trust is damaged.

If you trust someone, you believe them and would rather know the truth, even if they're confronting you about something. If you don't trust them, you want to avoid the conversation because you're not sure of their motives.

In a low-trust relationship, you're at a distinct disadvantage when you need to confront the other person. If at all possible, work on the relationship first. Take the initial steps to build trust with that person so confrontation will be more readily accepted.

The Simplest Way to Build Trust

Trust develops over time, not overnight. It's the cumulative result of little episodes of trustworthiness. The more a person engages in trustworthy behavior, the more trust grows. It's consistency that allows a person to take the risk of trusting you. In a sense, they're testing your actions to see if your behavior is just a performance or if it will stand the test of time.

Trust can be broken in an instant, and rebuilding it takes much longer. It's been said that it takes at least five trustworthy encounters to make up for one trust-breaking encounter.

One of the best tools for building trust is to listen to the other person without interrupting or steering the conversation. Listen in order to understand their perspective. If it's done in a genuine way, it impacts them deeply because it's so rare. It's the fastest path to a person's heart. Author David Augsburger said, "Being heard is so close to being loved that for the average person they are almost indistinguishable."[3]

● ● ●

In this section, we've been exploring the mindset necessary to have courageous, compassionate conversations. A healthy mindset is the foundation for success; now we need the right tools and techniques. Let's move into this next section of the journey.

PART 2

Becoming a Discerning Communicator

I'm a recovering perfectionist. I used to think perfectionism was a good thing, but then I realized it also made me a procrastinator. I wouldn't try anything new until I'd read multiple books and articles and watched online videos until I was absolutely sure I wouldn't fail. Failure wasn't an option; it had to be perfect. The only way to make sure that happened was, as my wife says, to "research until the cows come home."

That meant I rarely got things done. When I occasionally tried to accomplish something, I hit snags along the way. I'd go find another video to solve that problem. I justified my procrastination by saying I needed it to be perfect, and I wasn't quite ready.

When I was a kid, I wanted to learn to bowl. So I read a book on bowling and practiced the motions in my living room when nobody else was home. When I eventually went to a bowling alley, I wasn't perfect—so I gave up. At the same time, I realized that I'd learned more about bowling from playing for an hour than I did from all my preparation.

When I was a young adult, people occasionally asked me to join them for a game of golf. Before I agreed to join them, I read a beginners' guide to the sport. I thought I'd do pretty well the first time I played, but the windmill kept knocking my ball out of the way. I graduated to a real course, where the safest place for other people to be was directly in line with where I was trying to hit the ball.

Home repairs? I'd get a book. I wouldn't just look for the chapter on how to repair a leaky faucet; I'd start at the beginning and read about the history of faucets and how they'd changed over time. I figured that the more I understood about faucets, the more successful I'd be in repairing them. I'd also read about the different types of wrenches available and which would be most suitable for the job.

Usually, the repair worked, but it had taken me six weeks of study to stop the leak.

Then I met my future father-in-law. If his faucet leaked, he would turn off the water, grab the closest wrench he could find, and go to work. He'd dismantle the faucet to see if the problem was obvious. Then he'd go to the hardware store, get what he needed, and make the repair. An hour later it was done. It might not be textbook, but he fixed the leak—while I was still looking for articles on faucet repair.

He often shook his head at my approach to everything. The family was a water-skiing family, and it was expected that I'd learn how to ski. As they were planning my first outing, he said, "Now, don't go looking for a book on water skiing. I'm going to push you off the back of the boat, and you better hold on! And you'll need both hands, so you can't read while you're skiing."

Today, I'm doing much better at trying new things. I've learned that both approaches are needed and work best when they're used together. As my friend Jeff says, "Clarity comes from action." The best way to figure out how to do something is to start doing it. I might read a little to get some structure around the project, but now I jump in pretty quickly. It's only when I get stuck that I'll look up a solution online to solve my immediate problem. The research comes as the need arises, not before.

That will be our approach in this section. We'll look at the dynamics of how to communicate with courage and compassion, then we'll try it. It could be tempting to study each chapter until we feel confident, but the first conversation we have will provide challenges that weren't covered. Here's the best way to approach this content:

1. Read through the entire section quickly to get an understanding of how effective communication takes place.
2. Talk to someone and try out something you've learned.
3. Reread as appropriate while you're developing your skills.

That's it. Develop a bias for action, then follow it with research.

You won't get perfection. Instead, you'll see your communication skills grow, as well as your confidence in handling the toughest encounters.

Ready to get started?

5

Do I Have to Become Obnoxious?

Once you start disliking someone, everything they do is irritating to you.

Anonymous

Yesterday, I sat as an observer on a video call between two companies. One company had asked the other for a presentation of their services so they could decide if they wanted to work together. There were about a dozen people on the call, which was scheduled to last about ninety minutes.

After a round of introductions, one individual started going through the presentation to give an overview of what they were offering. She was polished and warm, engaging the group as if they were in a live classroom session.

About ten minutes into the call, one man interrupted her. "I'm sorry to break in," he said. "But could you go back and give me an agenda of what we're going to be doing on the rest of this call? It looks like you're teaching us some of the content, which is fine. But how long will this last—and what else will we be covering?" He continued, "I just need to decide if this is going to be worth my time or not."

You could feel the virtual air being sucked out of the room and see the shock on everyone's faces—especially his colleagues'. No one quite knew how to respond for a few seconds, because they weren't used to someone being that direct about what they were thinking.

Suppose you were on that call. Would you think he was rude or even arrogant? Or would you wish you could be that straightforward with what you were feeling? Perhaps a little of both?

I admit to having mixed feelings. My first response was, *What a selfish jerk. Isn't he aware of how he disrespected the presenter, alienated his colleagues, and hijacked the call?* I immediately wrote him off, and decided I didn't like him and wouldn't want to do business with him. But part of me secretly admired his ability to simply say what he was thinking. *I would never be able to do that*, I thought. *I wish it were easier for me to speak up without having to be so careful not to offend anybody.* There have been many times when I needed to say something but couldn't. In those cases, my silence came across as acceptance and approval when the exact opposite was true.

The Value of Genuine Assertiveness

The news reporter I mentioned in the previous chapter is skilled at what she does. She has developed her craft in a way that allows her to control the direction of almost any conversation. Whether I agree with her or not, I'm impressed. It's almost like watching a home-run champion hit a baseball, seeing a gifted artist paint, or reading something written by a master of words. I know it's taken her years to hone her skills to this point, and I'm fascinated by her precision.

She's good. She's skilled. And in the process, she is rude and obnoxious. I admire her abilities, but I don't want to be like her.

She specializes in intimidation and making people look worse than they might really be. She's aggressive and forceful, which makes for interesting television—but most of us wouldn't like to be one of her targets. We also wouldn't want to be her.

Why? Because most people want to have good relationships with other people rather than be intimidated by them. We want people to like us, and we want to like them. We'd like to be able to fine-tune our conversational skills so we have more courage to speak up when it's appropriate and also sense when we need to be more compassionate in our delivery.

There are plenty of courses and books on "assertiveness training," and people take advantage of them to build their confidence. That's scary for a lot of people, because they think it will demand they be more irritating and forceful in order to appear confident. They feel like nice people on the inside, but they believe the only way to succeed is to act tougher than they are.

Maybe you're hoping there's a way to build that confidence without becoming obnoxious. Or maybe you've noticed people respond to your words defensively, and you want to learn how to become more aware of the impact of what you say. Fortunately, that's exactly what we're going to do. To make that happen, we need to distinguish between becoming *assertive* and becoming *aggressive*. The difference is what will make confidence possible, regardless of your temperament.

Understanding Assertiveness

The easiest way to understand the difference between assertive and aggressive is to add a third element to the mix: being *passive*. Let's put them on a continuum.

Ride in the boat	Steer the boat	Capsize the boat
(Passive)	(Assertive)	(Aggressive)

Picture a group of people who rent a boat for a few hours on the ocean. They decide it will be a fun excursion together, and they pull away from the dock. Nobody's officially in charge, and there's no formal plan for where they're going to go. One person takes the wheel and begins to steer.

A couple of miles away from shore, the engine stops. No one checked the fuel before they left, and the tank is empty. It's the middle of the day, so they're not concerned they'll be "lost at sea." But there's a problem, and it definitely has everyone's attention. They need a solution. Nobody's cell phone works because they're too far away from shore, so they can't call for help.

It's been said that when you face a crisis, you lose your ability to keep up your image; the "real you" comes out. That's what happens on this mini-cruise.

Capsize the Boat

A few people are angry and upset at what's happening, and they immediately start blaming others for letting it happen. They're only concerned about what they're feeling rather than what others are feeling. They're *aggressive*, trying to dominate and control the group as they ridicule others' suggestions. When someone is that strong, it's usually a sign they're struggling with low self-esteem or fear and feel the need to force their way to the top. They'll throw out random ideas like, "OK, everybody grab a life jacket and jump into the ocean. We'll capsize the boat and set it on fire, and that'll catch people's attention and they'll come help us." They're on the far right side of our continuum, ignoring everyone else's ideas. They're uncomfortable with the situation and just want to become comfortable again.

Ride in the Boat

Then there are those people who know nothing about boats but came along because they were invited and it sounded fun.

They're passengers who've just come along for the ride, so they don't feel they have anything to offer in the situation. They don't want to risk saying something others might ridicule, so they keep their ideas to themselves. They're thinking, *Well, I saw a can of fuel in the back of the boat, and it seems like that might help. But what if I bring it up, and it's the wrong kind of fuel, and everyone makes fun of me? It's not worth mentioning.*

These are the "ride in the boat" people on the far left side of the diagram. They might have answers that could solve the problem, but they don't want to draw attention to themselves or risk conflict or ridicule. So they keep quiet and hope others figure it out.

Steer the Boat

In the middle are the "steer the boat" people. They're a perfect blend of the best of both positions; they're not intimidated by the forcefulness of the aggressive people, and they have the courage to bring up the issues that might otherwise be overlooked. They're solution-driven and caring. They're the ones who will engage others to see if any of them have ideas, which will lead to discovering the fuel can that will solve the problem.

The goal is to live in the middle of the continuum. It takes a blend of courage and compassion, saying what needs to be said while being considerate of the perspectives of others. Whether you're on the left or the right, the goal is to move toward the center. Passive people need to develop the courage to say what's on their mind without being intimidated by the reactions of others. Aggressive people need to become intentional about looking out for the needs of others by listening to their perspectives.

Moving toward the Middle

I've found that most people who would pick up a book like this are on the *passive* side of the spectrum. They're the ones feeling the most pain, because they desire change. They don't like being described as "passive," and they want to learn how to speak up when it's appropriate. They realize, though, that "passive" is an accurate description of them right now.

They might be people pleasers whose self-worth comes from the opinions of others. They can't risk someone not approving of them, so they keep quiet because speaking up might lead to conflict. They usually have strong opinions or perspectives they think would add value, but they keep those thoughts to themselves.

It frustrates them that they can't speak up because of fear but rather keep quiet and either gossip or tuck their feelings deep inside. Those feelings become toxic and grow, and that impacts their attitude toward life and the way they relate to others. Their primary technique, where they try to make everyone else comfortable and nobody gets upset, is like a pillow fight. It might be fun, but it doesn't make much of an impact.

They really want to move toward the middle, where they'll have the strength to engage with others and express their wants and needs with confidence.

Those on the *aggressive* side of the spectrum use strength and coercion to get their way with others. Their emotional attitude keeps meaningful conversation from happening, because they often ridicule or attack other people and their perspectives. They might also actively ignore them, implying their opinion isn't worth listening to. They're concerned with "winning" the conversation more than building the relationship. Their own needs become more important than the needs of others.

These people don't especially like the reputation that goes along with aggression, but it's all they know. They would like to have more meaningful relationships with people who would care about them, but they don't know how to make that happen. It's like their only tool is a club, so they use that club to manage every relationship.

Assertive folks are at the balancing point in the middle, where they're actually steering the boat. It's the "sweet spot" of communication: they have the courage to share their needs and thoughts in a way that meets the needs of others as well. This sets the stage for honest conversation that balances courage and compassion.

"But I do them both," you might say. "Most of the time I'm just afraid of saying the wrong thing and getting someone upset—or worse, I'll embarrass myself. But other times, I try speaking up and say too much, too loudly, or I'm confusing and people ignore me. I can't win."

You can win, and it's not that hard. There are two simple steps to move toward the middle:

1. Learn what it really means to be assertive and the value it has.
2. Take simple steps to practice assertiveness.

What Assertiveness Is and What It Isn't

To become appropriately assertive, we need a clear picture of what it looks like in its best form. Healthy assertiveness has these characteristics:

- You stand up for yourself and others. You observe what you're feeling, and you state it graciously.
- You focus on being genuine and speaking your truth graciously, regardless of the risk that someone won't like it. Their response simply shows who they are, not who you are.
- You're able to simply say no without explanation.
- You don't assume others are mind readers and know what you want.

- You hold people accountable for their actions instead of ignoring them because of fear.
- You see others as your equals rather than seeing yourself as above or below them.
- You're able to affirm others rather than try to change or "fix" them.
- If you need help, you can ask for it without feeling like it's a sign of weakness.
- You don't try to manipulate or harm others, and you seek genuineness in relationships.
- You pursue what you want while respecting others.

The biggest advantage of learning assertiveness is that it builds trust with others, which is the foundation for any healthy relationship. If you have multiple encounters with me in which you know I'm being truthful and honest, you begin to expect that from me. You relax because I'm consistent, and this provides the safety for you to be honest as well.

If you grew up without seeing it modeled, assertiveness can be uncomfortable. You might have been told not to offend people, even if it meant giving up what you needed. You might have been shamed into feeling selfish or rude if you asked for what you wanted and were told people wouldn't like you if you hurt their feelings. You became the peacekeeper so nobody would get upset. You learned to avoid conflict and to try to make it go away when it happened.

There's a better way.

Take Simple Steps to Practice Assertiveness

"OK, that makes sense," you say. "And I really want to live in the middle ground of assertiveness. I want to have the courage to speak up when it's appropriate and also to be sensitive to others instead of aggressive. But I've spent my whole life swinging from one side to the other. How can I actually begin to practice assertiveness in a way that lets me be myself?"

If you decided to run a marathon, you wouldn't go out and run twenty-six miles the first day. It would be so painful you'd give up and never try again. Instead, you'd start by walking around the block, then running a few steps, then building up your mileage and endurance over time. You would celebrate the little successes and enjoy seeing your abilities grow. Over time, your capacity to run longer distances would grow more than you ever thought possible.

It's the same thing with assertiveness. If you jump into a heated debate and demand your rights, you'll lose. It will be a painful loss, and you'll think, *See? It didn't work. I can't do this.* You'll give up trying because you just reinforced your perceived inability to do it. But if you start small and practice with little steps, it will soon become part of the way you operate. You'll gain confidence, and it will become a normal way of communicating.

To run a marathon, you first need to make sure you have the right shoes, the right clothing, a water bottle, a solid training program, and a coach. That's essential preparation. Then you can begin by taking the first step. For conversations, you've already begun that process. This book is your training program, and I'm your coach.

In learning assertiveness, the preparation starts with your mindset:

- Review often the value of assertiveness, as described throughout this chapter. Don't worry if you aren't feeling it yet, just reaffirm that it's true.

- Begin to see yourself as worthy of getting what you need and want. You're not more or less than anyone else, and you don't have to fix everyone.

- Visualize yourself being OK with other people not being OK when you're assertive. If they don't like the change, they might try to shame you with sarcasm or ridicule. Their response says something about them, not about you.
- You can't make someone else happy; that's their responsibility.
- Don't assume that when you start being assertive others will think you're being aggressive. It's possible, but it's rare. You're probably projecting on them your expectations of what they might be feeling. You might be afraid they'll think you're coming across as obnoxious, but they're probably not noticing anything at all. Check your intent; speak your mind with the right motives and value yourself.

Keep reviewing these principles daily. They might feel counterfeit at first but will soon become your reality as you keep them on your radar.

Once your mindset is in place, it's time to take the first steps. Remember to start small; you're just walking around the block for now, not running.

- Pick something simple that you want and ask for it. When a small group is trying to decide where to go out to eat, don't say, "Oh, I'm good with anything." Pick someplace you'd really like to go and state it. "I've been wanting to try that new Thai restaurant on First Street." You might get voted down, but it doesn't matter. You spoke up and shared your desire instead of just going along.
- Don't assume your spouse or a close friend knows what you want, as in, "They know me well enough that they should just know what I want for my birthday." They don't, so make a suggestion. "This year, I'd love to have the family grab lunch and bring it to the park."

- When someone doesn't do what they promised, don't let them off the hook by saying, "Oh, that's OK." Let them gently know what you're feeling. "Yeah, I was pretty disappointed you didn't come through on that. I'm sure it'll be better next time."
- Set realistic boundaries with people. If your mom keeps criticizing your spouse, just state that you won't participate in those conversations. "Mom, when you pull me into your frustrations with my spouse, it's not fair to either of us. I love you, but I'm not going to engage with you when that happens." She might press back by saying, "Oh, don't be silly. What about what they said at dinner last week?" Don't engage—simply repeat the boundary over and over again: "No, Mom, we're not going to talk about my spouse that way." No explanation, just repetition of the same boundary.

These are beginning steps, but that's all you have to do to get started. Try it with little things like these, and you'll find being assertive becomes natural over time. When that happens, you can stretch more.

The same is true in reverse. If you're more on the aggressive side, slow down and think before speaking. Consider how another person might be seeing a situation and look through their perspective before reacting. Watch how people respond to your words. Awareness will become the key to making an impact.

You don't have to become an expert all at once. Like running a marathon, everything we accomplish in life happens one step at a time. Reread this chapter as needed and determine what those steps might be for you, then focus on the first step and take it. Step one is the fastest way to get to step two—and then steps three and four.

Soon, you'll find yourself well along the path, feeling confident about your new, growing skills!

6

Overcoming Intimidation

I'm not short; I'm concentrated awesome.
As seen on a T-shirt

The first time I met the CEO of the company I work for, it was in the restroom. In fact, I've met the CEO of the last two companies I've worked for in the restroom. I've also met two well-known celebrities in hotel restrooms.

Each time, it was intimidating. I knew who they were, but I hadn't planned on running into them—especially there. I shouldn't have been surprised, because it's the one place everyone visits on a regular basis. When it happened, I found myself at a loss for coherent words. I wanted to make a good impression, but I have no idea what I said. In every case, after we'd walked out of the room, I immediately thought of at least a hundred different things I could have said instead of whatever I'd mumbled.

It doesn't matter how confident we normally feel; there are just some people who intimidate us when we talk to them. It might be their position, their personality, or their power. It could be someone who knows how to push our buttons and we don't know how to respond. It often happens when we're taken off guard and run into that person when we're not expecting to.

Why are we intimidated by some people but not others? Why do we get tongue-tied in their presence while we feel confident around others? *It's something that happens in our heads.*

Other people don't really intimidate us; they simply act in a certain way and say certain things, and it's up to us how we interpret those words and actions. Hard as it might seem, we can choose how we respond and how we perceive them. If we see them as better than us, it puts them "up there" while we're "down here." If we see them as the same as us, we're on level ground.

We're all different on the outside but the same on the inside. We're all human. Recognizing that is where we'll find the solution to being intimidated.

Playing on Level Ground

Usually, our friends, peers, and coworkers know us well. We've shared experiences with them, and we have a relationship. We've seen them at their best and their worst, and they've done the same with us. We've become comfortable with each other. We're not intimidated because we're equals.

It's usually people we don't know as well who tend to intimidate us. It might be a boss or a client, or it could be an authority figure like a police officer or a judge. To an introvert, it might be an extrovert. To an extrovert, it could be someone who thinks deeply and controls what they say so their words have great impact. It could be a well-known leader or a forceful family member.

We don't see them as being like us. There's no common ground, so we feel like we're on different playing fields. They're in the major league while we're in the minor league—or the other way around. If we know we're going to be meeting with them, anxiety hits. We feel like we're not good enough, or smart enough, or interesting enough to have a meaningful conversation that they'll find enjoyable, and we're already assuming we'll be embarrassed or they'll reject us. Or we might not see them as interesting, so we don't value them (especially if we see ourselves in the major league and them in the minor league).

So, are all those thoughts true?

It doesn't matter. *Whether they're accurate or not, our thoughts become our reality.* We act on our beliefs.

The problem is we're comparing our lives (which we know) with their lives (which we don't know). Comparing our reality with our *perception* of their lives is like comparing apples to giraffes: it doesn't even make sense. If we got to know them, we'd start to see their flaws, their struggles, and their fears. We'd see they wrestle with parenting issues and finances and other people *they* find intimidating. We'd see them as real people with real issues that are simply different from ours.

In other words, we'd see their *humanity.*

I once heard someone say that the reason we struggle with insecurity is we compare our "behind the scenes" perspective with everyone else's highlight reel (and it happens the most on social media). We compare our chapter 1 with their chapter 20, our real life with our contrived impression of their life.

We need to check the truth about our thoughts. Anytime we feel intimidated, we should write down what we're believing in that moment and ask, "Is it true?" When someone tells us we're stupid or inadequate for a task, we rarely challenge their perception to see if it's accurate. We just internalize it and assume it's true. Instead, we can simply think, *Am I really stupid? I don't know everything, and there are things I don't know very well. But there are a lot of practical things I do know well and things I can do well. I'm not stupid; that's just a label they gave me, and I don't have to accept it or believe it.*

We can talk back to our thoughts. Correcting those negative thoughts takes away their power over us. If we don't challenge our thoughts, our minds believe them and our bodies react to them.

Whenever you feel intimidated by someone, stop and remind yourself what's true:

- Am I intimidated by what they *said* or by what I *think they mean?*
- They're not better or worse than me. They're human.
- Their opinion is exactly that—*their* opinion. It doesn't say anything about the real me.
- When I'm focusing on the negative, I need to remind myself of the positive.
- I shouldn't assume I know what they're thinking. I need to explore to find out.
- I don't have to compare myself with them and become like them; I just need to be myself.

Make It Practical

Imagine you will certainly run into your company CEO in an elevator or meet a local celebrity at the grocery store. Decide ahead of time what you could say, instead of scrambling for words on the spot.

What should you say? Most people try to think of some way to impress the other person. That usually backfires because you're focusing on how you're coming across instead of the other person. Think of something they've done or said recently that made an impact on you, then simply thank them for it. Be genuine and precise and make it about them—not you.

Less effective: "I really enjoyed your presentation last week."

More effective: "Last week in your presentation, you talked about the early failures you had in your career. That was refreshing, and I think we were all energized by your honesty."

Less effective: "I watch you on the news every night. I'm so happy to meet you."

More effective: "When you're reporting stories about crises, you have a calm demeanor that gives us all hope. Thanks for that."

Less effective: "Thanks for having us all over. We had a great time."

More effective: "That was a fun evening. It was great watching the way you connected people based on their interests so they had something to talk about."

Notice the difference? We're used to saying the same simple things everyone else says, which has less impact. But what you say will have more impact if it's specific and concise. It doesn't have to be profound; just pick something they have said or done that had genuine meaning to you, and thank them for it.

I met legendary comedian Carol Burnett a few years ago at a book signing she held at a local bookstore. I heard everyone in line telling her the same things: how much they loved her, how long they had been watching her, and how funny she was. She was very gracious in responding, even though she must have heard the same comments thousands of times throughout her career.

When I had the chance to connect briefly, I simply said, "Carol, you've brought a lot of joy to our family over the years. Thanks."

She paused, looked me in the eyes, and smiled. "Well, that was very kind of you. Thank you for saying that. It means a lot."

Whether it's a celebrity, a person of power in your life, or simply the people you're closest to, the power of simple, honest gratitude is amazing.

Ways to Overcome Feeling Intimidated

It's easy to assume that we'll always be intimidated by certain people because they're just intimidating. They have an aggressive style or a position of authority, and we can't think quickly enough to know how to respond. If we're waiting for them to change, it's not going to happen. The change comes inside of us: how we view them and ourselves, and how we choose to respond.

Who comes to mind first when you think of intimidation? Ask some of these questions to analyze what's happening inside you:

- What insecurity do you recognize? It could be a feeling that what you have to say isn't important, or you're often misunderstood, or you're powerless.
- What stories do you tell yourself about that person?
- What do you believe about them and your relationship?
- What do you believe they think about you?
- Are those stories and beliefs true? Or are you assuming they're true?

Don't look for long, exhaustive answers. Notice your first thoughts in the moment. Instead of automatically believing those thoughts and internalizing them, learn to do a "belief scan" and challenge what you find. Now consider these perspectives, especially when you find yourself on the receiving end of some-one's aggression.

Don't Withdraw

When people say things about you that are unkind or un-true, it's natural to internalize those statements. You're hurt, but you don't say anything so others will think you're tougher than you feel. You put up a wall by not letting anyone see who you really are, so nobody can hurt you. When that happens, it drags you down emotionally, drains your energy, and makes it tough to think clearly when you need to. Yes, the wall keeps the pain from reaching you, but also the love. It's not worth the trade-off. Practice using those initial feelings as a trigger to remind yourself what's true instead of automatically accepting their words as accurate. Don't let their comments define who you are; it's their opinion, not a diagnosis.

Look for Truth

People can't intimidate you without your permission. When they attack, use that as a trigger to reframe what they're say-ing. Don't assume it's true just because they said it. Recognize that what they said expresses what they think, not who you are. Don't allow their words to change your reality. Quickly and mentally challenge what they've said. Ask yourself, *Is that true?* Then determine the accurate mindset you should have.

Apologize If Needed, but Don't Grovel

Sometimes when we're intimidated and make a mistake, we tend to say "I'm sorry" over and over. Humans make mis-takes, so an apology is appropriate and welcome. Apologize sincerely, be specific about it, and keep it short—then move past it.

Reinforce Your Value

We can't eat one big meal and expect it to last for an entire week. In the same way, it's important to remind ourselves often the truth about our value. When we're not feeling valuable, we're more susceptible to being intimidated because we see ourselves as "less than." So we should make it a practice—perhaps daily—to think through an accurate perception of our worth. It's not just reciting affirmations to make ourselves believe something that's not true; it's reviewing what is true.

Carry Yourself with Confidence

When you're feeling confident, it's natural to stand up straight and walk tall when entering a room. When your confidence is lagging, you're inclined to slump and slink through the door. Before joining any gathering, check your posture and reflect confidence in the way you stand. It's not a "fake it till you make it" technique. It's a conscious decision to reflect physically what you've determined to be true mentally. When people see you walk with confidence, they'll assume it reflects what's inside. If they see you slouch, they'll assume things about that as well.

Remind Yourself That You're Enough

You don't have to become more than you are in any situation and pretend you're more confident than you feel. Confidence comes from being fully and completely yourself in any situation. It's OK to work on your conversational skills and connecting techniques. Realize, though, that there's nothing you can do that will add more value to who you already are. You are enough because you're you.

Don't Be Afraid of Failure

You're not putting on a performance that's being graded. You're learning by doing. You'll have some encounters that go

93

better than others, and you'll wish you had phrased some things differently. But instead of beating yourself up over it, look at it as a stepping-stone. Learn from the experience and use it to move ahead to the next stage of competence.

Confidence Is in Your Head

CEOs and celebrities are human, just like us. That should be obvious since I met them all in a restroom, a place that everyone visits. There's common ground between all of us, and there are plenty of ways that's true beyond the restroom.

How do we overcome intimidation? By balancing our common ground (how we're alike) with our uncommon ground (how we're unique). It involves getting a clear, accurate view of how we're alike and how we're different—*and seeing them both at the same time.* Balancing our humanness and our uniqueness keeps us from comparing. We become free to be who we are without having to become something we're not.

My CEO turned out to be one of the warmest, most caring, and most high-integrity people I've ever met. His business acumen is off the charts, and he's proven his competence and built trust. He cares deeply about everyone in the company, no matter what role they play—and won't hesitate to connect with anyone who needs a boost.

When we're intimidated, it usually stems from our incorrect perceptions. Changing our confidence comes from changing our mindset. We recognize that we're not stuck in the way we relate to others; we can take practical steps to see ourselves— and others—in a new, realistic way. Then we become intentional about practicing that perspective day by day. We will no longer cower when someone lashes out at us but will be able to see what's happening without intimidation.

How refreshing would that be?

7

Words That Work

Words are free. It's how you use them that may cost you.

Anonymous

June in Southern California is mockingbird time.

As we sat on the patio for dinner, a mockingbird serenaded us. I'm always amazed because they have so many songs in their repertoire. They've been created with the amazing ability to "mock" other birds, duplicating up to two hundred different calls—loudly and clearly.

It's the avian version of a Kindle. You can store hundreds of birdcalls in a single device. Mockingbirds are easy to spot, because you can just listen for the sound and look for the tallest point around, like a tree or roof peak. That's usually where the sound is coming from.

I did a little research and found out that for the mockingbirds it's all about romance. Most often, the males make the most noise, trying to attract the attention of the females. That's why they land where they do; they want to be seen easily, and they want to be heard. They're not shy about advertising their presence. (Ladies, you're probably thinking this sounds like some guys you've known, right?)

During the day, I'll often take my work outside so I can hear the concert. For me, it doesn't get much better than that—listening to a bird do exactly what it was created to do and doing it well.

But there's a problem: they sing at night too. At 3:00 a.m. I'm not nearly as amazed. Their song isn't soothing when I'm trying to sleep. It's still well done, but I don't care. I want it to stop. It's like the neighbor who's playing loud music in the middle of the night. The only sound you want to hear is the sound of silence.

The Cost of Words

We have a lot of things to say, using words we think others will want to hear. Sometimes, those words are exactly what they need and are appreciated. At other times, those good words are spoken at the wrong time or in the wrong circumstances.

> We give advice when someone just needs our presence and a listening ear.
> We focus on our own problems without noticing someone's pain.
> We talk about the tough stuff first thing in the morning when they're a night person (or vice versa).

Some people are more talkative than others, but it doesn't mean they have more words. It just means they let more of those words out than quieter people, who keep their words to themselves. It's not that we lack words; we just have trouble deciding which ones to use in a given situation.

Having lots of words is like having an expensive set of razor-sharp kitchen knives. When used in food preparation, they allow us to make precise cuts to get the exact results we need.

If they become dull, it also becomes easier to cut ourselves instead of the food. Imagine cutting through a firm tomato. If the knife is sharp, it slices easily through the tough skin without any pressure. If it's dull and we have to apply pressure to make the slice, the blade could easily slide off and cut our finger.

Words are like knives. If they're carefully chosen and kept properly sharpened, they can precisely fit the conversation to get great results. If they're casually tossed around, somebody's going to get hurt.

We grew up with the saying, "Sticks and stones may break my bones, but words will never hurt me." While that sounds good, it's not accurate. Our words can cause great damage—or great healing, depending on how we use them.

That old saying could be an expression of someone who has been hurt by words so many times that they've developed a tough exterior to protect themselves. Words don't hurt them because they've walled off their feelings, not because the words themselves have no impact.

This is an important chapter in our quest to communicate with courage and compassion. Words are the building blocks of conversations, and we need to learn how to use them with precision. Sometimes we're intimidated and can't think clearly, and we wish we had the courage to think quickly enough to say the right words. When that happens it's natural to blurt out something to fill the void—and we end up using words that confuse or hurt, and we regret what we've said. It's like we're playing with our knives and somebody gets hurt. Sometimes we hurt others; sometimes we hurt ourselves.

The Power of Casual Words

When we were first married, Diane and I lived in a tiny, rented cottage in Redondo Beach, California. It had been built in 1920, and our landlady had renovated it just before we moved in.

The garage was too small for our cars to fit, so we always parked in the driveway. Part of the charm of the house was that driveway—two strips of cement with hard-packed, rocky dirt between them. We could almost picture a Model-T Ford with its skinny tires resting on those narrow strips. The black ground in the middle was almost as hard as the cement, soaked solid from decades of oil dripping from various engines and mixing with the dirt.

Diane's first job was as a preschool teacher. Every evening we would sit together on the floor in our little living room, cutting and pasting and creating activities for her next day's class. I was amazed at her ability to build experiences that would shape a tiny little person's understanding of a key concept.

One day we collected a popcorn maker, a bag of popcorn, and a bunch of paper cups. In class, she popped the corn with the lid off, so each "pop" would send fluffy flakes flying around the room. Each kid had a little cup and the task of racing around trying to catch the popped kernels before they hit the ground. (I don't remember the point, but it sounded like an amazing activity!)

She pulled in the driveway at the end of that day and opened the hatchback of our little Honda station wagon. The leftover popcorn kernels had spilled while she was driving, and some fell out onto that grimy, rock-hard strip of dirt. It was only a few kernels, so she left them there as not worth picking up. We didn't think about those kernels again.

Until they started to grow.

First, it was just little green sprouts. Then the plants took on the distinct appearance of corn. We parked in the street so we could watch the progress. Within a few weeks, tiny ears of corn began to appear. They never reached full size, and we definitely didn't harvest and eat them. (We weren't sure what kinds of toxins from that soil might have made their way into the corn.) But we were amazed that anything could grow there.

I try not to force everything that happens to me into a life lesson. But for some reason, that one has always stuck with me, and it reminds me of how we drop words all the time without even thinking. Whether those words are encouraging or discouraging, they fall into the lives of everyone we meet. We never know when they're going to take root in someone and make their life better or worse.

Has someone ever made a casual remark that changed your life, and they didn't even know it?

I've gone to powerful conferences, read great books, and heard well-crafted sermons. Somebody had an agenda for me, and I willingly participated. I took notes, read between the lines, and studied the concepts so I could apply them to my life. Marketing people have thought carefully about the letters they've sent me, and salespeople have tried to convince me their products could change my life. In every case, the word choices were intentional. The presentations were designed one slide at a time. Books were written thought-by-thought. Letters were penned with a purpose.

When I look back, though, the words that have changed my life the most have been the unplanned, casual ones someone never planned to say and doesn't even remember saying. These unscripted words have filled my tank when it was running low, turned my steering wheel when I was drifting, and put the right address in my GPS. They reminded me why I was on the journey in the first place.

Their speaker is usually someone I've learned to trust. We have a relationship. They didn't always know what I was going through, but they said something casually—unknowingly— that hit me exactly where I was. Their words changed my life, and I still carry them years later.

Once in a while such unplanned words have hurt me. The person wasn't intentional or malicious, and they might have been joking. But their words cut deep. I probably didn't tell them, and they didn't know my pain. Yet I have carried their hurtful words for years too.

That's why it's critical to pay attention to the words we use. If we want to have courage and compassion in our conversations, it starts with being intentional about what we choose to say. I've learned several things from the impact casual words have had on me:

- My casual words impact others more than I might realize.
- Most of the time, I don't even know when it happens.
- If you're smiling, I'll assume you're OK. I could be dead wrong.
- I don't know how my words are impacting you, because I might not know what you're going through right now.
- My words have the power to hurt.
- My words have the power to heal.

Knowing the power of casual words, why would I take the risk of hurting someone just to be clever or make someone else laugh at their expense? I want my default setting to be words that *affirm*. It takes practice, but I want to be intentional with my words, whether crafted or casual. I want my words to always carry this message: *I believe in you.* Why? Because we all have times when we don't believe in ourselves. When that happens, we need to borrow that belief from someone else.

A Talking Society

We're a noisy society. Everybody's talking and nobody's listening. Turning on the television or spending time on social media exposes us to everybody's opinions. If people feel like they're not being heard, they get louder and act more confident and post more often. But if it's all talking and no listening, what's the point?

Too many people are like mockingbirds. They're talking all the time, sharing their opinions from the rooftops, hoping to attract the attention of anyone who will listen. The result? People can become irritated, not inspired or helped.

Someone said that God gave us two ears and one mouth for a reason. In fact, King Solomon (in the biblical book of Proverbs) reinforced the importance of timely communication:

"You can persuade others if you are wise and speak sensibly" (16:23).

"Fools have no desire to learn; they would much rather give their own opinion" (18:2).

"It's stupid and embarrassing to give an answer before you listen" (18:13).

"A kind answer soothes angry feelings, but harsh words stir them up" (15:1).

"There is more hope for a fool than for someone who speaks without thinking" (29:20).

We all think we have important things to say, and that other people need to hear them. That's probably true, but taking the time to listen and explore someone else's perspective gives us an audience with them. It builds trust and credibility and earns us the right to share—and helps us discern which words are the most appropriate in the situation.

The Words of a Confident Communicator

"Your call is important to us. Please hold for the next representative."

What's your reaction when you hear those words? You're probably thinking, *If you really thought my call was important, you'd have someone pick up the phone and talk to me.* Companies carefully craft words like these to make us want to trust them more, but they often ring hollow and are transparent, and they have the opposite effect.

Have you ever been talking to your spouse or a close friend about something important, but they seem a million miles away? They might say all the right words ("I'm listening. . . . That makes sense. . . . Yes, I'm paying attention. . . . Whatever you decide is fine"), but you feel like you've gotten a recording that says, "All of our representatives are busy."

We can't automate our communication. How can we become more intentional about what we choose to say? It's a matter of thinking through the words we're about to speak and answering these questions:

- Do they meet the needs of the listener?
- Do they simply and clearly present my position?
- Are they kind?
- Are they accurate?

That's how simple it is. Instead of blurting out something and hoping it comes across well, slow down enough to craft what you want to say. Remember, your words are like a scalpel, and you're the surgeon. It's your responsibility to think about the impact of your words before you use them.

Here are a few examples of words that communicate with both courage and compassion.

"I Was Wrong"

I was absolutely sure the roofers would paint the trim boards they had to replace. "They wouldn't leave a job unfinished," I confidently said to my wife, who believed we would have to do it ourselves. I was frustrated that she couldn't understand the obvious, which made it even tougher when the roofer said, "No, we don't do any painting."

I could have ranted about the business and how it made no sense. But my relationship with my wife was more important than my relationship with the roofer. I took a deep breath and told her, "You were *so* right, and I was *so* wrong." It was that simple, and we were OK.

Strong people admit when they're wrong, which builds trust. Weak people ignore their mistake or defend it, which weakens trust.

"Tell Me about It"

It's easy to say, "How was your day?" or "How was the meeting?" But since the other person can respond with a one-word answer, it feels routine and disengaged. Instead, say, "Tell me about your lunch with your friends today," or "What decisions were made in the meeting?" Those open-ended questions show you were listening and allow them to share the details. Listen carefully and ask clarifying questions.

When someone begins to tell you about something that happened, slow down, look them in the eyes, and say, "Tell me about it."

"Help Me Understand"

Tough conversations start with a difference of perspective. The other person isn't you, and they have their own way of seeing things. Many people argue by repeating their position louder and louder but stop listening when the other person is talking. They're busy planning what they'll say when it's their turn.

When you feel anger, frustration, or intimidation rising during a conversation, slow down and say, "Help me understand." Set aside your agenda and listen without interrupting or planning your reply. Ask clarifying questions without adding anything to what they're saying. If you just let them talk, they'll see your focused attention as a gift—and will be more inclined to do the same with you. "Help me understand" is a phrase that de-escalates tough conversations and opens the door to genuine trusting connection.

What's the common thread in all of these phrases? We're listening instead of just talking.

Talking is using our words. Listening allows us to use the other person's words.

Bring those together, and our communication becomes a powerful blend of courage (talking) and compassion (listening).

That's the foundation for *real* relationships.

8

Feelings as Fuel

I wish I was full of tacos instead of emotions.

Anonymous

When I was a teenager, I read a book about how to handle emotions. It had practical suggestions for dealing with the feelings a teen might have, and the ideas seemed helpful and made a lot of sense.

The book suggested that there were two emotions that seemed to have the most impact on conversational skills: anger and fear. They were both described negatively as something unacceptable in any situation. Anger was bad because of the damage it did when you're upset and because it made others uncomfortable. Fear was bad because it was a sign of weakness and would allow people to walk all over you. The book implied that strong, negative emotions were something we needed to ignore, control, or suppress. I was young enough that I wasn't able to discern if it was right or wrong, so I just believed it. After all, it was in a book, right? It must be true.

It also made sense to my teenaged mind, because I had experienced both emotions firsthand. I watched other people lose their temper in a group setting and embarrass themselves. I realized that when people were trying to have a logical discussion but it started getting emotional, logic went out the window. The more I witnessed that happening, the more I wanted to avoid it.

I had times when I felt something strongly and wanted to speak up but didn't have the courage. I was afraid of people's reactions and what they would think of me. I wanted people to like me, so I made sure nobody ever saw me as angry or afraid. I believed that emotions were wrong because they caused so much pain, so I stuffed mine down inside and simply became "pleasant." Nobody told me there was another side to emotions.

That pattern continued for several decades. All those emotions I had tucked away were not gone but rather growing inside. After a while, they began creeping out in subtler ways such as sarcasm or resentment.

Fortunately, I eventually learned about a different perspective on emotions: they could become fuel to drive powerful conversations with great results. Strong emotions weren't something to get rid of; they could be tools in my toolbox to help me become more confident in my communication.

I needed to change the way I saw emotions and learn how to use them well.

You can't simply stop a strong emotion any more than you can conjure one up at will. If I said, "OK, I want you to be really frustrated right now," you'd think I was crazy. It's the same if I said, "Be really happy." We don't pick our emotions in the moment; they just appear automatically as a result of what we're thinking. We might not be able to stop feeling, but we can challenge and change our thoughts at any time.

Fear of Heights

Have you ever assumed something about another person that made you angry with them, but then found out it wasn't true?

Your emotion came from your belief, which came from what you were thinking.

The 103rd floor of the Willis Tower (formerly the Sears Tower) in Chicago has an observation deck with a balcony you can walk out on and stand on. This balcony has a glass floor. They say it's perfectly safe, but you're looking straight down at the street below.

Would you walk out on it?

On the 70th floor of the US Bank building in Los Angeles, you can step out of the building onto a forty-five-foot glass slide that takes you down to the 69th floor. The glass is one inch thick.

How about that one? Even if you weren't afraid of heights, I think it would at least get your attention. It might be exciting because it has the scent of danger. That glass is supposed to be stronger than the average floor, but somehow it seems riskier.

Why? It's all about how we think. Our emotions in that moment come from the way we interpret what we see in that situation.

A couple of years ago, I led a meeting in an executive boardroom on the top floor of a skyscraper. When it was time to leave, I started to step into the elevator—something I've done thousands of times without ever giving it a thought. But this time, as I stepped inside, I glanced down. A shaft of light was shining up through the crack between the metal strip on the elevator floor and the one on the building floor.

The lights had been left on in the elevator shaft.

Through that thin opening, I was able to see the open shaft going down seventy stories below me. Near the bottom it was dark, which made it seem like an eternal dungeon. I realized I was stepping into a small metal box held up by a single cable. Once I was inside, that cable would be lowering me down that shaft toward the darkness.

I stepped in and pushed the "lobby" button. The doors closed, just like always. The familiar beige music played, just like always. I felt the drop—the same as always.

But it wasn't the same. I had seen the light and knew what was below. All of those thousands of times before, I never questioned what I was doing. Nothing had changed in the experience; the difference happened in my head. All those other times, I never considered the danger. This time I was focused on it and felt the fear.

It's amazing, isn't it? The things we think about have a way of determining our emotions. The reality doesn't change, but our thoughts and perceptions do. When our thoughts change (for good or for bad), that changes how we feel.

We're often told changing our lives involves changing our actions. There's some truth to that, but it's not the main issue. Changing our lives happens when we learn to first think differently, which affects our emotions, which determine our actions.

As Shakespeare wrote, "There is nothing either good or bad, but thinking makes it so."[1]

- Your teenage son agreed to be home by 11:00 p.m. It's 1:00 a.m. and he hasn't called. You don't know what's happening, but your mind goes to the worst-case scenario—right? When he finally walks through the door, your fear evaporates as it is replaced by anger.

- You've heard rumors at work that downsizing is coming. You don't know if the rumors are true, yet they take over your thoughts. It doesn't take long for you to imagine losing your home because you can't make the payments.

- You feel a pain you haven't felt before, and it worries you. You haven't seen a doctor, but you can't help imagining a debilitating disease. Soon you're not imagining it; you're believing it to be true.

- A friend at church passes by without saying anything to you. In reality, they were lost in thought and didn't see you. But you spend days wondering what you did to offend them.

How can we take control of our thoughts instead of letting our thoughts control us? By observing them and challenging them. We need to take notice of our negative thoughts and talk back to them, evaluating them to see if they're realistic and true.

Pastor and author Max Lucado suggests a great metaphor for controlling our negative thoughts—the ones that keep us up at night:

> You can be the air traffic controller of your mental airport. You occupy the control tower and can direct the mental traffic of your world. Thoughts circle above, coming and going. If one of them lands, it is because you gave it permission. If it leaves, it is because you directed it to do so. You can select your thought patterns.[2]

Your problem might not be the only problem; it's the way you think about your problem. Your thoughts make up the ingredients of your emotions. To learn to use emotions properly in conversation doesn't mean you don't let any planes land; you simply determine which ones land, in which order, at the proper time.

Pay attention to your feelings during the next few conversations you have. Notice when there's emotion involved and what the emotion is. Use that as a trigger to examine and engage with your thoughts, challenging them: Are they true? It won't solve every issue you encounter, but it can turn your mind in new directions.

Keep in mind that we're not talking about "quick fix" solutions in this chapter. We're talking about changing our mindset and making choices. When there have been profound hurts over years or a lifetime, those scars could run deep. In those cases, we can't just read our way out of them. We need to enlist the skills of a professional therapist who is trained and experienced in dealing with that type of trauma. If we had a brain tumor, we wouldn't do the surgery ourselves; we'd get the best surgeon possible. It's no different with our emotions.

Do People Enjoy Being with You?

If we rolled all of our emotions into a ball, they would blend together to form our *attitude*. Our attitude impacts how we relate to other people in our lives. It's the foundation for being able to gain courage to speak up in tough conversations, and it also sets the tone for learning to bring more compassion into our dialogue.

We could take each different emotion and analyze it in the context of how it impacts our relationships. For our purposes here, though, let's think of them together under that umbrella of *attitude*. Attitude describes how others see us and how much confidence we have relating to them.

The dictionary describes *attitude* as "a settled way of thinking or feeling about someone or something, typically one that is reflected in a person's behavior."[3] Notice the pattern? Thoughts lead to feelings, and feelings impact behavior.

Some people have a positive attitude about life. It's not a fake, syrupy kind of positivity, just a general optimism that's contagious. You feel better about yourself when you're with them. When you're in a conversation with them, you don't want it to end. It feels safe to share yourself in that environment.

Other people are generally negative about life. No matter how good something is, they tend to find the downside. Spending time with them can be draining, and you're often looking for a way to end the conversation.

Here's the big question: *Which type of person are you?* When people spend time with you, are they hoping the conversation will continue, or are they looking for an early exit?

It's All about Attitude

Most people live a reactive life. If good things happen, they feel good. If bad things happen, they feel bad. Their emotions depend on their circumstances rather than on their mindset. They're like a ping-pong ball on the ocean, drifting wherever the waves take them.

It doesn't have to be that way. We all face the same variety of circumstances, but we don't have to be at the mercy of those circumstances.

We can choose our attitude.

Two people are in the same traffic jam, riding in the same car, late for the same meeting. One person is anxious and upset and stressed; the other person is calm. What makes the difference? They're thinking different things and coming to different perspectives about the same situation. It's how they choose to respond.

You likely have seen this popular quote from pastor and author Chuck Swindoll:

The longer I live, the more I realize the impact of attitude on life. Attitude, to me, is more important than facts. It is more important than the past, than education, than money, than circumstances, than failures, than successes, than what other people think, say, or do. It is more important than appearance, giftedness, or skill. It will make or break a company . . . a church . . . a home.

The remarkable thing is that we have a choice every day regarding the attitude we embrace for that day. We cannot change our past . . . we cannot change the fact that people will act in a certain way. We cannot change the inevitable. The only thing we can do is play the one string we have, and that is our attitude.

I am convinced that life is 10 percent what happens to me and 90 percent how I react to it. And so it is with you. . . . We are in charge of our attitudes.[4]

My father-in-law has that quote hanging in his bedroom. It's become his paradigm about life, and I've heard him quote it many times over the years. When my mother-in-law had a stroke, this mindset shaped the way they faced the journey together.

Our attitude is fluid, not fixed. We can choose to change it. When we do, it gives us exactly what we need to blend courage and compassion in our most challenging situations.

How to Change Your Attitude

James Allen wrote, "Every action and feeling is preceded by a thought."[5] The thought comes first, then the feeling follows. If we want to change our feelings and emotions, we start by changing our thoughts.

The key to changing our attitude is to change our thoughts. King Solomon said, "As he thinks in his heart, so is he" (Prov. 23:7 NLV). We become what we think about.

Want to become a different person—someone people are attracted to because of your attitude? Pay attention to your thoughts. When you're feeling negative, stop and ask yourself these two questions:

1. What are the facts in this situation?
2. Can I do anything to change the situation?

If you can do something to change the situation, take action. If you can't change the situation, learn to accept and adapt.

Caution: this advice can sound trite to someone who's struggling with clinical depression or experiencing overwhelming grief or life issues. Those are different issues and require a focused therapeutic response. In this chapter, we're talking about people who have simply developed a chronic pattern of negativity because of the way they think.

Ten Intentional Steps for an Attitude Adjustment

Truly positive people aren't pretending to be happy; they're being realistic. They don't allow themselves to become victims of things they can't control, and they put their energy into the things they can do something about.

Is it time for an "attitude upgrade"? Try exploring these ten options.

1. **Know where you're heading with your life.** When you have a clear sense of purpose, you'll know where to put your energy. You'll be able to make choices that move you forward and set aside the things that stall your progress.

2. **Learn to find satisfaction in the present, but keep moving toward something new.** Make "flexibility" your mindset so you're always open to growth opportunities.

3. **Move from "expectation" to "expectancy."** If you're looking for a guaranteed result when you take action, you'll often be disappointed. Expectancy means you do something, then watch with anticipation to see what happens.

4. **Change the way you look at failure.** Instead of avoiding failure, see it as a step of growth and learning. Author John Maxwell says you should "fail fast and often."[6] Don't let failure stop you; just see it as one more checkmark in the process of succeeding.

5. **Hang out with positive people.** It is often said that you become like the five people you spend the most time with. Seek out new relationships with people you admire, and spend less time with those who drag you down. Obviously, we live with our family members and might spend the most time with them. We're talking here about expanding our outside relationships to include the healthiest people possible, no matter what's happening at home.

6. **Take yourself lightly.** Spend less time thinking about yourself and more time thinking about others. If you're always worried about what others are thinking about you, relax. Realize that they're probably not thinking about you at all. Most people are focused on themselves, not others.

7. **Don't expect others to live up to your standards.** Trying to change others keeps you frustrated. Accepting others as they are frees you to be yourself.

8. **Develop a lens of gratitude and look at all of life through it.** Look for the bright side of every situation. When storm clouds have a "silver lining," it's because the sun is shining behind them. The clouds might be ominous, but the sun is real.

9. **Stop comparing yourself with others.** If you use somebody else's life as your rule (especially on social media), you'll always fall short. Everyone's at a different place in life, so it's unfair to compare. Measure your growth against where you used to be and where you want to be. Use your own yardstick, not theirs.

10. **Make decisions, then make them right.** Make quicker decisions, knowing that not everything will turn out the way you plan. Life is meant to be lived, which is tough to do if you spend all of your time playing "what if."

Changing your attitude doesn't happen all at once. Growth happens when you tweak one thing in the right direction, then others over time. If you do it in community with others, being accountable and intentional allows growth to happen exponentially.

Try a few small steps to grow your attitude, then see how it impacts your confidence in communication. By working on your thoughts, you'll see a change in your feelings. You'll discover new skills in building genuine relationships and have much greater confidence in your communication.

9

The Power of Silence

I wish more people were fluent in silence.

Anonymous

You go to a theater to watch a movie. You sit through all the previews of upcoming attractions and ads for popcorn, candy, and soft drinks. Maybe you're interested, maybe you're not—but you're part of a captive audience. If you're sitting with friends, you'll keep talking until it's time for the movie to begin. Then the lights are turned down and the music is turned up—your signal that the main event is starting.

The final clip you see is a brief one that says, "Please turn off your cell phone." The basic message is, "Something important is about to happen. Pay attention. Don't make any noise or do anything to distract others so they can pay attention too." And in many theaters, the clip ends with three words: "Silence is golden."

Wouldn't you like to have that clip to show before some conversations you have? Or some meetings you attend?

We've all been in situations where some people are talking over each other while others sit quietly—not because they have

116

nothing to say but because they don't know how to get a word in edgewise. The talkers don't want to leave any space between their words, for fear of somebody else jumping in. The quiet ones are frustrated because there are lots of words but no content. It's just noise to them.

Author Susan Scott described a weekly one-on-one meeting she had with a senior executive who was her coaching client. Invariably, he talked nonstop and monopolized the conversation. She wasn't able to provide the direction and counsel he was paying her for because he never left space in his monologue. One day, she simply stood up and headed for the door. "Where are you going?" he asked. She replied, "So far, we haven't had one-on-ones. We've had 'ones.'"[1]

Everyone has ideas to share, and everyone wants to be heard. If nobody is listening, it's tempting to talk more and louder. There's still no content, just competition. When silence happens, it's like a vacuum that grows stronger until somebody fills the void with words. The longer the silence, the more uncomfortable we become.

In reality, silence is one of the most powerful tools a person has to bring depth into a conversation. For someone needing more courage to speak up, mastering silence provides a way to enter into tough conversations. For someone who can't stop talking, silence is a way to get others to listen. You're building trust because you're showing interest in other perspectives.

It seems counterintuitive, but when it comes to words, less is more. Mark Twain reportedly once wrote to a friend with this apology: "I didn't have time to write you a short letter, so I wrote you a long one instead."[2] Using lots of words without being intentional is easy. Communicating concisely takes more effort but has a much greater impact.

Friedrich Nietzsche said, "It is my ambition to say in ten sentences what everyone else says in a whole book."[3] He understood the power of silence.

Why We're Afraid of Silence

I once heard someone say that most people are so uncomfortable with silence that if their car's radio and air conditioner break at the same time, they'll get the radio fixed first. They'd rather deal with the summer heat than the silence.

Why do we tend to see silence as negative?

When we think of silence in a meeting or conversation, we often add the word *awkward* before it. If the silence goes on too long, we feel like we have to say something—anything—to break the tension. The tension is uncomfortable, and nobody likes to be uncomfortable. At the same time, we crave silence when someone is talking nonstop and we can't get away.

A few years ago, I was flying into an airport late at night that had a noise curfew—meaning that flights couldn't land there after 10:30 p.m. However, my flight had been delayed before takeoff on the other side of the country, and the landing was going to miss the deadline. So we were rerouted to another airport about thirty miles away. To get us to our original airport, the airline planned to put us on shuttles that held about ten people each. That took about an hour to arrange. We boarded the shuttles around midnight, and everyone was tired because of the late hour and the long flight. The drive would take about forty minutes.

One person sat in the front seat and took advantage of the opportunity to engage the driver in conversation. He talked nonstop, primarily trying to convince the driver to convert to his particular faith. He wasn't having a conversation, because the driver wasn't responding. The man was just monologuing, and it was loud and animated. Every time it got silent, he filled the space with another idea.

All of us were tired, and the last thing we wanted to hear was someone talking nonstop—but no one had the courage to say anything (including me). I was in the back seat with another man. At one point, he leaned over to me and quietly said, "Do you think God would punish me if I killed him?" He was joking, but his frustration was obvious.

The reason we're afraid of silence is that we've usually only seen the negative side of it:

- We were sent to our room as kids for "quiet time" and saw it as punishment because there was no one to talk to.
- If we're silent in a meeting or other conversation, we're afraid we'll be seen as not having answers or anything valuable to say.
- If we don't say something, someone else might jump in and say what we were thinking, and they would get credit for our ideas.
- When someone else gets quiet, we might assume we offended them. If we don't talk more about it, we go away thinking the other person doesn't like us or is angry with us. In most cases, the opposite is probably true; we just believe our negative thoughts.

When someone is quiet, it's easy to make assumptions about what they're thinking. We believe those assumptions, then start behaving as though they are true. That's dangerous. The only way to really know what someone else is thinking is to ask them.

Author and psychotherapist Richard Joelson described a dialogue between a couple in his office:

Sue, someone who is always anxious about her appearance, asks Tom after ten minutes of complete silence on date number three, "Is there anything wrong?" feeling quite certain that he must be displeased with her looks. Tom replies, "No, not at all. I was just thinking about how much I have enjoyed our time together and how much I like you and was trying to figure out a way to tell you without sounding too mushy."[4]

119

Assuming that silence is always negative ignores the possibility of it being a valuable asset in conversation.

What's So Good about Silence?

When we talk about silence here, we're referring to it as a tool, not a weapon. It's not being frustrated with another person and being unable or unwilling to tell them. It's not about avoiding conflict to dodge an argument. That's using it as a weapon. We're talking about how silence can be a resource for building genuine relationships. It's about being aware of exactly what's happening in a conversation in the moment.

One of the things we learned from the COVID-19 pandemic is the value of spacing. We learned that putting six feet between ourselves and others would keep bad things from happening between us. Also, wearing masks would keep toxic stuff from transferring between people.

Silence is like that. It provides "spacing" in our conversation where everything can slow down. When our conversations slow down, we're not just cramming words over other people's words to fill space. We're allowing more time to think. We're taking time to process what someone else is really saying. We can also observe their body language and pick up meaning through their tone of voice. Silence is the mask that protects us from the germs of impulsive speech, allowing us to use "on purpose" words that lubricate the conversation.

Talking *with* people instead of *at* them lets you review what you believe about something before you answer. It protects you from saying an impulsive yes to something you really want to say no to but can't think of how to say it—because the conversation doesn't have space.

The best part of this space is that you get to be yourself, which is your greatest strength. You're not posturing or manipulating or impressing; you're just *being*. It will help you be relevant in what you say, it will make it easier to genuinely pay attention, it's a simple way to strengthen relationships, and you'll feel energized when it happens.

Appropriate silence in a conversation slows down the dialogue and allows people more space to think. It takes a little courage, and it will feel uncomfortable at first. And it's a priceless skill you can become proficient at with just a little practice.

Practicing the Skill of Silence

How do you feel when you're alone with no noise or media? If it's uncomfortable, it's time to take tiny steps to experience its value. Begin with something as simple as taking a walk in the park without your headphones. You might feel overwhelmed with thoughts, and it will be hard to relax. Don't make it a power walk for exercise; just take a stroll and see how many sounds you can hear that aren't manmade. The traffic, sirens, and other human sounds will still be there, but listen past them for the birds, water, and wind that can only be heard when you're intentional about finding them.

Practice that until it becomes comfortable. You'll begin to find the value and joy in the quietness. When you do, you'll start to have reasons to build silence into your conversations.

Seasoned salespeople understand the value of silence, while novices force the conversation along their scripted presentation. The toughest thing to learn is to ask a question and let the customer respond, but then refrain from saying anything for a few seconds. It seems like an eternity, and the customer will feel that uncomfortable void as well. If the salesperson stays silent, the customer almost always jumps in to break the tension. When they do, they often volunteer more of their thoughts, ideas, and preferences than if they were just answering question after question.

It's tough to try at first, but the results are almost always amazing. That applies to everyday conversations as well. Instead of forcing ideas when there's a little pause, just let the silence sit there for a while. Savor the rest, and just notice what comes up naturally. Generally the thoughts will be much deeper because they were allowed to grow in the silence.

In this way, silence becomes a simple technique you can practice quickly and see the results of immediately. In any encounter, don't feel compelled to keep the conversation going all the time. If the dialogue slows down, just let it. Use silence to slow a conversation down so you can have a rich, meaningful exchange of ideas.

If the other person keeps rushing to fill the voids, that's OK. Be an observer instead of a player, and pay close attention to how they're communicating. You'll begin to recognize another person's conversational skills when you don't feel the need to compete. Listen to what they're saying without having an agenda, then ask a meaningful question when it's appropriate. You'll be talking less and can learn to enjoy a less-pressured conversation. Your conversations become deeper, you don't have to appear clever, and you won't have to resort to giving advice. Your conversational priority becomes understanding, not speaking.

Silence gives you time to reflect. Reflection gives you time to formulate good thoughts, which provides the raw material for great conversations. You'll be able to speak with substance rather than show off your speaking skills.

The first few times you try it, you'll think, *They said something or asked me something, and I'm supposed to stop and process? Won't that seem weird? Won't they wonder why I'm not responding?*

For one thing, it will seem longer and more painful for you than it does for them. We're not talking five minutes of silence; it could be as little as three to five seconds. It might feel like an eternity, but it gives you time to pull your thoughts together. In that amount of time, the other person won't notice the pause; or if they do, it will just be getting on their radar by the time they hear your next words.

It's perfectly OK to say, "Let me think for a second about that—I want to process before I respond." That gives you permission to take even more time to think and also communicates the reason for your silence. The other person will also recognize that you're listening enough to take time for careful thought, so your reply will have more impact. It's not a gimmick to just buy some time; it's a way of giving your full attention to the process and engaging more thoroughly. It shows that you care.

When Is Silence Appropriate?

Think about these scenarios:

- During a conversation, the other person stops talking. You sense they might have more to say, but they seem to be hesitant about sharing it. Is it better to bring it up and explore, let it ride and hope everything is OK, or just sit in the silence and let them know they don't have to speak until they're ready?

- You're talking to a service company about the price being requested, and you know it's negotiable. It feels uncomfortable to ask for a lower price, but you also know it's more than fair. Could you ask for that price and wait for their response, or would you simply accept their position? And if they don't budge, could you say, "Well, this needs to feel right for both of us. It seems like we're at an impasse, so it's probably not a deal we should make," and then wait for their response?

- A coworker disappoints you because they didn't do what they promised you they would do. Do you admit you're disappointed, which might lead to them becoming defensive, or would you stay silent about your frustration and say, "Oh, that's OK" and ignore it?

- In a conversation, someone says something that is hurtful or causes you to become angry. Would you respond to it and risk the conflict escalating, or would you remain silent about your anger and not say anything?

There are no easy answers to these scenarios because every situation is different. Here's what's most important to remember:

- Silence is a tool.
- There are times when that tool is appropriate to use, and times when it's not—depending on the situation.
- You aren't required to use silence, but if it's not in your toolbox, you won't have it as an option.

Confidence in conversation comes when you grow your ability to use silence to become free from communication chaos.

10

How to Change
Someone's Mind

We all have the ability to change the lives of others,
but only when we lose the fear of changing ourselves.

Rohan Kallicharan

How many times has this happened to you?

You're scrolling through Facebook and see a post from someone who's presenting their side of an issue you strongly disagree with. They describe the "facts" of their position, citing recognized experts to show that their argument is accurate. In so many words, they're saying, "I'm right, you're wrong, and here's why." You see their logic, and you instantly give up your position and adopt theirs. You think, *Well, now that I've seen the facts, I realize that I was wrong. I've changed my mind because of what they said.*

My guess is that the answer is "zero." In fact, you probably had the exact opposite response, and it reinforced your original position. After reading such a post, you feel stronger about your own position than you did before and are less likely to change.

On social media, we see people weighing in on important issues by carefully explaining why their position is right and everyone else's position is wrong. There's usually a lot of energy and emotion in the threads—and the longer those threads grow, the more heated they become.

Someone said, "If the only tool you have is a hammer, every problem becomes a nail." In social media, we only see one tool being used: *logic*. That's fascinating, since none of us have changed our minds because of those logical presentations. Logic just doesn't work.

Why do we keep using it? Because it's all we know. People use "facts" to convince, thinking that a logical presentation will do the trick. After all—if a person doesn't change their mind after seeing facts, they're ignoring the truth. They're just being stubborn, right? Deep inside we think, *What's wrong with you? Facts are facts, and you're just ignoring them.*

But with social media, "facts" aren't necessarily true. They're just presented dogmatically, as if to say, "Well, everybody knows this is true." If you and I are using facts that disagree, we're both convinced that *our* facts are accurate (even if they're different). If I believe my facts are accurate, the problem must be with you. You're thinking the same thing about me—and our dialogue comes to a standstill.

For most people today, "facts" are no longer trusted. It's like seeing a photograph that is supposed to prove something, but we've seen so many digitally altered photos that we can't tell what's real and what's not. When facts can't be trusted, logic becomes irrelevant.

Using facts to change someone's mind is just like throwing punches at them. If someone was about to hit me, I wouldn't just let the blows come; I would instinctively put my hands up to defend myself—or punch back.

Sounds like social media, doesn't it? The same thing is true in real, everyday relationships too. Other people think differently than we do, and it drives us crazy. Our spouses can be stubborn, our teens often act subhuman, our toddlers are selfish, our friends can be needy, and our coworkers are insensitive. We want to have healthy conversations with them, but it can be tough. When they hold strong positions and won't budge, we might get intimidated because we don't know what to say. If we're irritated, we blurt out our own version of facts and logic to show that we're right—which just makes it worse.

Is it possible to change someone else's mind? Well, yes . . . and no. If we're only using facts, it won't happen. We've all heard the definition of *insanity*: doing the same thing you've been doing over and over and expecting different results. Since facts and logic alone don't work, why would we continue using them?

We need a different approach.

What Does It Take to Change Our Minds?

We don't like to be wrong. Without our even trying, our minds are constantly on the alert for information and input that reinforce what we believe and reject things that don't. We pick news channels we agree with. We read a blog that supports our perspective and share it with others. We're drawn to things that let us think, *See? I'm right*. If something doesn't support our views, our minds set it aside as irrelevant.

This is called *confirmation bias*. It means that when we want something to be true, we end up believing that it is. When we've collected enough information to support what we want to believe, we stop looking at evidence. That includes anything we might see that's contrary to our beliefs. We've formed our opinions and stop thinking about any other options. It's a form of self-deception, because anything that goes against our opinions is seen as a personal threat.

I'm writing this several months before a major US election. The rhetoric is heated as candidates present a carefully crafted image while viciously attacking their opponents. Since I'm thinking through this while I'm writing, I'm seeing my own biases at work. I believe I'm objective, but I'm not. I find myself unconsciously seeking positive news about the candidates I favor and negative stories about the ones I don't. If I was truly objective instead of just reinforcing my current beliefs, I'd seek out details and facts that might impact my perspective about who to support.

A self-confident person is willing to look at evidence that's contrary to what they believe. They're not threatened by other perspectives because they want to explore what's true. They still hold to their own beliefs but aren't defending them against those views. Instead, they welcome and explore other perspectives, knowing they will either reinforce their beliefs or make them worth changing.

They might still believe they're right but aren't threatened by the possibility of being wrong—or at least finding they can fine-tune their position.

Did you notice the key element in that description? They're *willing* to challenge their beliefs, not be forced to do it. Changing their minds starts with their own openness to the possibility of change, not a barrage of facts and figures from an opponent. That means that I can't change your mind on anything. All I can do is influence your willingness to do it yourself.

What does that look like?

You're Dealing with a Person, Not a Project

In the 1970s, Dr. Frank Wesley, a psychology professor from Portland State University, studied a group of competent, loyal US soldiers who were captured during the Korean War. We might expect they held firm to their loyalty to the United

States while they were in the prison camps (even though those camps were known for using torture as a way of changing a prisoner's loyalty). But this group willingly defected to North Korea—not because of mistreatment but because they were unexpectedly treated with kindness. Peter Boghossian tells the story:

> His research showed that virtually all of the defectors came from a single US training camp. As part of their training, they had been taught that the North Koreans were cruel, heartless barbarians who despised the United States and single-mindedly sought its destruction. But when those POWs were shown kindness by their captors, their initial indoctrination unraveled. They became far more likely to defect than those POWs who either hadn't been told anything about the North Koreans or had been given more neutral accounts of them.[1]

These soldiers had been indoctrinated with facts and had been given a seemingly bulletproof understanding of the enemy. But the North Koreans didn't try to convince them how wrong they were; they simply treated them as people, not enemies. The result? The soldiers changed their minds. They got a new experience that didn't match the old information, and they made new, unexpected choices.

What can we learn from this experience that we can apply to helping others think differently?

1. **Don't rely on "facts."** Human kindness does what logic can never accomplish. In the face of compassion, facts become irrelevant.
2. **Don't argue.** When you argue, you're questioning the other person's judgment. The more you establish a genuine connection, the more likely they'll be to consider your perspective.

3. **Build a real relationship.** The people we have genuine connections with are the ones we trust enough to listen to. If we try to convince without having connection, we're treating them as a project. It usually means we don't care about them; we're just concerned about winning the debate and being right.

4. **Be a model of good behavior.** You can't control the way they behave, but you can demonstrate an alternative. When you do, it's contagious.

5. **Entertain the possibility that you could be wrong, at least to some degree.** Keep an open mind about every topic, even if you're confident of your position. It's the only way you'll be able to truly listen for understanding, which builds trust in the relationship.

6. **Be a partner, not an adversary.** Winning arguments is worthless if it doesn't make both people better. Always have a mindset of caring.

You can't set out to change another person's mind. That's their job. If you build a connection, you build trust. When you have trust, you can talk honestly about real issues—and both of you might fine-tune your perspective.

Separate the Person from the Issue

Over the years, I've blocked a few people on my Facebook feed. They're usually people I've known and "friended" in the past but don't know very well now. Over time they've taken on a different online persona, hotly defending their positions on various subjects and spewing venom at those who disagree. (Have you noticed that people can be much more abusive in writing than they are in person?) If someone takes a different perspective, they don't just attack that perspective; they attack the person as well.

We do the same thing when someone cuts us off in traffic. We don't know the person, but getting cut off makes us angry, and we assume the other driver is aggressive and uncaring. That's a real possibility, but we also could have simply been in their blind spot and they didn't see us. Since we don't know them, we judge their character and assume they're just a bad person.

Judging others based on our own assumptions is a dangerous approach; it dehumanizes others because of what they believe or do. We don't separate the issue from the person and feel that the only solution is to convince them they're wrong. That's when we pull out the "attack facts," which only reinforce their position.

However, when we separate the person from the issue, we can see the value of the person in the midst of the disagreement. If we dislike someone, it will be tough to influence them. We'll just want to change them. The place to start changing anyone's mind is to value the person and separate them from the issue.

When we're talking about how to change someone's mind, we're most concerned about doing so with the people we're close to. That's where we have the most influence and where the stakes are highest. Facts and logic mean nothing unless they're in the context of a high-trust relationship.

Here's an example. Several years ago, my wife and I had a disagreement. It was about money (isn't it always?). We discovered that people don't argue as much about things they have in abundance. Diane and I have never had a disagreement about air because there always seems to be plenty to go around. However, if we were trapped underwater, air would be the only thing we would think about. When something gets scarce, it gets our attention and emotion. So when money becomes scarce, it's a focal point.

When our disagreement started, we shared our feelings about the issue. We couldn't find a resolution, so we put it on the back burner for a while. Then we got busy and didn't talk about it, even though it was simmering in the background for both of us. We found ourselves feeling a low-grade irritation with each other as the days passed. It wasn't just the money anymore; it was personal.

A week later, the issue bubbled back up to the surface, and it was time to talk. Money had driven a wedge between us, and we were missing each other. We had spent the week mulling over who was right and who was wrong, but not talking about it. The issue was pushing us apart.

We reconnected, affirmed our commitment to each other, and then dealt with the issue together. Here's what we learned: *we needed to put the issue on the outside so it pushed us together, not between us where it pushed us apart.*

When volatile issues show up and disagreements happen, they almost always appear *between* two people, right smack in the middle. When that happens, the other person becomes the enemy—the problem to be solved. Two people who care about each other start fighting each other instead of fighting the issue.

We need to fight the issue. Issues show up in every relationship, so we can't wish them away. What should we do when they show up?

1. Remind each other that the relationship is more important than anything else.
2. Agree that the issue is the problem, and you need to attack it together.
3. Express emotions genuinely without attacking the other person. Stick with "I'm feeling this" instead of "You did that."
4. Realize that the issue might not be resolved quickly. Turn it into a project to solve together and commit to finding a creative solution that involves both perspectives.

5. If there's no resolution, agree to disagree agreeably. This shows you've separated the person from their position, which allows you to relate with courage and compassion.

When Diane and I finally reconnected, we sat in the car and talked through our emotions and how we both perceived the issue. We reaffirmed our care for each other and our relationship. We realized that staying connected was more important than who was right or wrong, and it was the only way to face the issue together.

That was several years ago. We still disagree and haven't completely resolved our money issues. But we still like each other, and we're in this together.

People over Positions

Issues are sneaky and deceptive. They always try to convince us that they're not the problem.

They're lying.

Always make the *issue* the problem, not the person. Relationships are a team sport. Move the issue where it belongs, and you can work as a team.

This chapter is called "How to Change Someone's Mind." At first glance, most of us might say, "Well, that's obvious—you already told us that you can't change anybody's mind. It's up to them." That's true if we're using facts and logic, like most people do. But in a genuine relationship with high trust, people are open to change.

My wife and I have changed our minds on a ton of things over the years because we wanted to. I'm a different person because she cares, and we still disagree on many things. We've learned that happiness comes from our relationship, not from being right.

There's a much better chance of changing someone's mind—and them changing yours—if you know they care. That doesn't happen when you're arguing on Facebook; it happens in person. (Someone said that the best way to have productive arguments on Facebook or Twitter is not having arguments on Facebook or Twitter.)

Want to change someone's mind? Maybe it starts with the willingness to change your own.

11

How the Right Questions Build Confidence

He who knows all the answers has not been asked all the questions.

Confucius

———

Want to know a foolproof technique for having people think you're smart? Here it is: don't talk. It's true, even if it's not practical. If you don't talk, two things will happen:

1. You won't say anything you could later regret, so you'll never need to backtrack or apologize. That solves the problem of saying the wrong thing at the wrong time.
2. Everyone will assume you're confident and have a good helping of wisdom. King Solomon said, "Even fools seem smart when they are quiet" (Prov. 17:28).

When someone talks a lot, others may think they're just chattering without thinking. If someone is quiet, others might see them as being so sure of themselves they don't need to spout their opinions.

The problem is that when we have something we want to contribute, keeping quiet is frustrating. In this book, we're trying to learn how to communicate with both courage and compassion—speaking up when it's appropriate and refining what we say so it has the greatest impact. How can we become proficient in our conversations when we're still building our skills, especially when we have trouble thinking of what to say under pressure?

There's a simple, overlooked technique that's often used by the best communicators but ignored by others: asking questions.

When we're struggling to communicate effectively, we think, *I need to learn how to converse better.* In our minds, that translates to better *talking* skills. Unfortunately, that pressures us to choose our words more carefully and think more quickly in the moment. The responsibility for maintaining the conversation is all on us.

But if we can hone our skill of asking powerful questions, even the quietest person can set the tone of any conversation. Instead of having to come up with clever things to say, we can use questions to explore the depths of what the other person is thinking. It allows us to take the entire conversation deeper.

This is not a technique for avoiding conversation, because we can't just ask question after question so we never have to give our own opinions. It simply allows us to build a framework for others to talk, and we'll be able to add our perspective as appropriate.

It's kind of like moving a car down the road. If you feel responsible for saying the right things throughout the conversation, it's like you're behind the car, pushing it down the road. It's possible for a while but eventually becomes exhausting. When you become an expert at asking the right kind of questions in the right situations, you've jumped into the driver's seat and are steering the car. It's not exhausting and allows you to set the destination and make the turns that will get you there.

If you're someone who has been pushing your whole life, this is a refreshing approach to conversations that will give you a whole different level of confidence in any situation.

Building Your Question-Asking Muscles

Most of us believe we're right about just about everything. It's not necessarily because we're prideful or arrogant; it's just that our perspective is clear to us. Over our lifetime, we've had different inputs that have shaped what we believe. If something seems crystal clear to us, it's tough to understand why someone else would see it differently.

The other person believes they're right too. Their perspective might be different, but it's just as clear to them as our perspective is to us. If we're in a conversation with someone and both of us think we're right, we may start using facts and data to show the other person why they're wrong. That turns a normal conversation into a debate where the result will be a winner and a loser—not a stronger relationship.

It's as if one person is describing a house from the front, where it's been designed to look like a high-priced mansion with perfectly manicured landscaping. The other person is describing the same house from the back, where the paint is peeling, the lawn has been ignored for months, and the patio is in disrepair. Both people see the house clearly and can't understand why the other person doesn't see the same thing. They're shouting back and forth over the roof to convince the other person they're wrong.

Asking good questions can change that entire dynamic. Instead of focusing on what you're seeing and describing it, asking questions allows you to walk around to the back of the house to see what the other person is seeing. You're exploring their perspective by standing next to them, not yelling at them. Then you both walk around to the front of the house and repeat the process.

When this happens, we don't have to have all the answers. We're not trying to prove that the other person is wrong but rather to understand. We can both be 100 percent right about what we've been seeing, but now we can expand our perspective with new information. The right questions allow us to grow and learn together.

That requires humility but builds relationships. We have to take a completely honest look at our communication skills to see if we're yelling over the roof or walking to the other side of the house.

How can you tell what your conversation patterns are? Consider these four ideas:

1. Keep track of how frequently you make statements in your conversations instead of asking questions. Pay attention during several conversations you have throughout the day, maybe even writing down what you observe. Then analyze what you've discovered. Are there certain times, people, or topics where or with whom you tend to talk instead of explore?

2. When you're in a conversation, pay attention to what you're about to say. If you're going to make a statement or give your opinion, see if you can turn it into an open-ended question (where they can't just give a yes or no answer). Instead of, "They need to rethink the entire project," you could say, "What do you think they should do to get better results?" Instead of, "You should take some time off to relax," you could ask, "What are some things you might do to feel less overwhelmed?"

3. Plan a conversation ahead of time where you will prioritize asking questions instead of making statements.

You don't have to be obnoxious, just experiment and see how many questions you can ask before making a statement. Notice how it feels and how it impacts the outcome of the conversation.

4. If you realize you just gave a lot of opinions in a conversation, acknowledge your error and ask a question to improve it. Perhaps you could just say, "I gave you a bunch of suggestions about how you should handle that tough relationship. But I realize that might not help, since you're much closer to the situation than I am. What do you think would be a realistic option?"

Asking World-Class Questions

You might think you're going to need to carry a "cheat sheet" of dozens of questions to ask people to get a conversation going. And there would be some value in that, because it would help you be intentional when you engage with someone. But for most conversations, the process is a lot simpler. If you learn three specific types of questions, you'll be able to do some true exploration with anyone—and you won't have to be clever or quick. Consider them a framework you can apply in any conversation, one that's totally flexible no matter which direction the conversation goes.

Here's the framework, and you'll use each type of question in order:

1. **Initiate with open-ended questions.** Avoid yes or no questions when you're talking through issues. That gives the person a chance to give their thoughts and opinions instead of just responding with one-word answers. Just ask some version of, "What do you think about this?"

139

2. **Follow up with deeper questions.** Once they've given you the basic information and shared their thoughts and perspective, don't let it drop there. Simply say, "Tell me more." That way you're leaving it open for them to take you deeper. Continue exploring with other versions of that same question:

   - "What else are you thinking?"
   - "What would that look like?"
   - "How would you measure that?"
   - "How would it make you feel?"
   - "What concerns do you have?"
   - "Is there anything else?"

   You don't have to plan these questions ahead of time. Just listen to the person carefully, then ask different versions of "Tell me more."

3. **Clarify with a review question.** A great way to make sure you're on the same page is to summarize what they've said and ask if it's accurate. "So, let me see if I'm getting this right. Your position is [summarize what they've said]. Is that accurate?" It gives them a chance to say yes if you got it right. If you didn't get it right, they can clarify their position as needed. Once they've done that, you can resummarize to make sure you're both on the same page.

The purpose is to find out exactly what the other person is thinking. Most people ask someone a question and accept the first response as the total answer, but this expanded process adds value because it allows you to go beneath the surface to get the details of their thoughts. It brings clarity instead of assumptions and helps people communicate accurately and avoid misunderstandings.

You won't use this in every situation, but it's a simple tool when you want to get clarity on a person's perspective.

How Old People Can Teach Us to Communicate

We tend to believe we're objective most of the time. But have you ever made a decision about someone just by looking at them? You don't know anything about them, but you make assumptions based on their race, gender, age, or behavior.

You feel comfortable more quickly when someone is just like you.

If you like someone, you might assume everything about them is good.

The experience you've had with a group of people in the past becomes the way you view one individual who is part of the same group (for example, if the group seemed lazy, you might assume every individual in that group is lazy).

You treat wealthy people differently from homeless people.

Here's an age-related example. Let's assume you're working with a person who is either twenty years older or younger than you. If they're older, you might assume they aren't good with technology. If they're younger, you might assume they're addicted to technology. Neither may be true, and those assumptions might get in the way of discovering the truth.

That's when it's valuable to ask questions to explore their experience and perspective, setting aside any preconceived ideas.

I experienced this several years ago when I played Scrabble with an eighty-eight-year-old woman who spoke English as her second language. I'm pretty good with words, and I do pretty well with Scrabble. I assumed she wouldn't have a chance.

I lost. Miserably.

My daughter's in-laws had invited us over for Thanksgiving, and the game was an after-dinner tradition. So Angie (my opponent) and I sat at the table and lined up our letter tiles. I

141

went first and proudly placed the first four-letter word that jumped out at me.

She emptied her tile rack on the first play, which included a double word score. I thought it was just a lucky move, but she repeated the pattern throughout the game. I would play my little words, and she would play her big words.

I don't remember the final score. But I remember being amazed at her skill. When I asked how she got so good at Scrabble, she humbly said, "Oh, I guess I've always been pretty good at word stuff." She told me about growing up in Mexico and how her family often played board games.

I forgot her age. She was just a person—like me, like all of us—in an eighty-eight-year-old body. She might not be up on the latest technology and might have a more traditional outlook on life. But we were on the same journey; she was simply further down the path than me.

It occurred to me that I could learn something from people who'd already traveled the path I have ahead of me. It's like getting a travel guidebook when exploring a new country that gives you an overview of what to expect. I don't have to do everything that's in the book, but it gives me a place to start and highlights to look for. Without the guidebook, I might miss some of the most amazing features because I'm ignoring the experience of others who've been there before.

If two people spend an entire conversation talking at each other, they're just exchanging thoughts to impress each other. If they're curious enough to ask genuine, caring questions, they can discover things that will add richness to both of their journeys—and build a relationship in the process. Neither person has to give up their viewpoint and adopt the other's perspective. They can just explore their positions in order to understand, not to convince.

It might be easy for me to unconsciously assume things about Angie because of her age, but I'd miss out on that richness.

Older people are often ignored because we assume they're out of touch, old-fashioned, and stuck in their ways. But I've learned that the opposite is often true. They have wisdom that comes from experience, but they won't force it on someone who doesn't value their perspective—and so we miss out.

Older people used to be teenagers. They had struggles with school, with dating, and with self-esteem. They argued with their parents, negotiated with teachers, and navigated first jobs. They had skills and awards and activities that brought them to life. They danced and sang and played. They had dreams. They had their hearts broken. They loved, lost, and survived.

Now, time has passed and they face the challenges of aging. But on the inside, they're the same person. They've lived through life and figured it out. We can learn from that. We don't have to walk their same journey, but we can gain a perspective that can be priceless.

Talking to older people is one way you can practice asking questions, but it can apply to any relationship. Here's what it might look like:

- Spend unhurried time with them.
- Ask specific questions about their life:
  - What was dating like when you were a teenager?
  - What did you usually do after school?
  - What kinds of things were you passionate about?
  - Tell me about your first job.
  - What kind of relationship did you have with your parents?
  - What were you afraid of growing up?
  - What would you do differently if you could live your life over again?
- Listen carefully as they talk. Ask clarifying questions.

- Ask them about a challenge you're facing with your relationships, your job, your health, or your plans for the future: "What would you do if you were me?" You don't have to do exactly what they say, but you'll gain their perspective.

That's the magic of asking questions. You're steering a great conversation, getting a ton of things to talk about, learning things you'd never otherwise know, building a strong relationship—and you don't have to have any clever things to say.

Keep It Simple

It's tempting to think of only using these questioning techniques in the tough conversations where we feel intimidated. But I've found that they apply in pretty much every situation. I've used them with kids, grandkids, teenagers, toddlers, coworkers, friends, and just about anyone else I talk to. The purpose is to increase your conversational skills—not your talking skills, but your skill in exploring another person's position. It means walking to the other side of the house.

Don't overplan this, just practice it. It has to be genuine, coming from your honest desire to understand their perspective. If you're using it as a ploy to make them think you care, they'll spot it a mile away. Remember: you're striving for a relationship, not a debate.

Try it this week. Experiment with a few questions in your next few conversations and see what happens. I can't give you any guarantees, but I'm confident you'll be amazed. You'll think differently.

It could totally renew your confidence in every conversation!

12

Outcome-Based Conversations

If you don't know where you are going,
you might end up somewhere else.

Yogi Berra

———

Years ago, my friend Steve and I sat in the back seat as our hosts drove us through the countryside surrounding Addis Ababa, Ethiopia. They were living there as missionaries and knew the area well. Steve also had been there many times, but it was my first experience in Africa. I peppered them with questions about what I was seeing, trying to deal with the sensory overload.

As we drove, I saw a number of huge, rusted-out tractors sitting in the middle of fields. Curious, I asked why they were there and where they had come from. Our host, Dave, described the scenario.

"Several years ago, a group of generous Americans came over and asked the farmers what they could do to help," he said. "The farmers said they needed oxen to plow the fields. The Americans went home and decided that they wanted to give them more than that, so they bought tractors instead and had them shipped. They assumed it would be an 'above and beyond' gift to show their generosity."

He continued, "The farmers were gracious and grateful for the gift. But they couldn't afford the gasoline and didn't know how to maintain them. They were experts at animals, not machines. So the tractors have been sitting abandoned in the fields ever since."

It's easy to be critical of the Americans who thought they knew what was best and didn't listen. If you asked them what the purpose of their trip was, they would probably tie it into their generosity. They had more resources than most people, so this was an opportunity to use those resources to help others. They wanted to be generous, so giving the tractors was an extreme expression of that generosity. Their purpose was to *give*.

The only problem was that the gift didn't meet the needs of the farmers. It met the Americans' needs. The farmers needed more resources to plow their fields, but the well-meaning Americans tried to meet that need by looking at it through their own perspective. It was a noble effort, but the outcome came up short.

What was the *real* outcome that was needed? It wasn't tractors. It wasn't even oxen. The desired outcome should have been to give the farmers what *they* needed to produce a successful crop. If that had been a clearly focused outcome from the beginning, every decision could have taken them to that end.

Someone once said that a builder doesn't buy an electric drill with a ¾-inch bit because they want a ¾-inch bit; it's because they want a ¾-inch hole. The hole is the outcome; the drill bit is what makes it possible.

Most conversations are the same way. Casual conversations are comfortable touchpoints with people you know well. But in an important or challenging conversation, the place to start is with a clear idea of what you want to accomplish. Without that clear outcome in mind, it's easy to talk in circles when the pressure is on. If you know where you're headed in a high-stakes conversation, you can evaluate what to say (and what to avoid saying) to get the results you want.

What You Can Control in a Conversation

"But that doesn't make sense," you might say. "A conversation is too fluid and unpredictable to try to steer it in a certain direction. You never know what the other person is going to say or how they're going to respond."

That's 100 percent true. You can't control all the unknowns in a conversation, and there are plenty of them. Trying to corral the whole thing is like trying to use logic with a teenager: it can be futile and frustrating. But you don't need to control everything in a conversation. There's only one thing you have control of: *you.* You can make choices for how you approach a conversation, where you're heading, the things you say, and the way you respond. You can have a distinct purpose for each conversation that impacts what you say and do, not what anyone else says or does.

It's really just deciding, *Why am I having this conversation? What would I like the outcome to be?* Figure out what you want to accomplish and why it's important to you, and that becomes a GPS for your side of the conversation.

Determining your purpose is a combination of two things:

1. Your confidence in yourself.
2. Your relationship with the other person.

Your Confidence in Yourself

Your confidence is not arrogance but a deep sense of who you are and what you believe and value. The more secure you are in yourself and your position, the less threatened you'll be by other people, no matter how they come across. It's not about fixing, rescuing, or changing the other person. It's about being your unique self. Your uniqueness is your greatest tool in any conversation.

When you feel confident, you won't be intimidated by another's knowledge, personality, or approach. You'll be able to observe the dynamics of the conversation instead of getting sucked into the issues. That frees you up to stay focused on that outcome.

Your Relationship with the Other Person

Not all conversational partners are created equal. We could probably put them all on a continuum to determine our purpose. One end is *transactional*, while the other end is *relational*. There will be overlap, but here's how it works.

On one end are the people you talk to who you don't have much of a relationship with. It could be a barista at a coffee shop, a delivery person who brings packages to your front door, or the person who inspects your house for termites once a year. In these situations, your purpose will be mostly *transactional*: getting the right beverage, obtaining your package safely, or getting rid of little wood-munchers. It's not a deep, long-term relationship, so your purpose will be to have a smooth transaction.

On the other end are the people you are closest to in your life, those you have a long-term commitment to because you interact with them often and do life together. This can include your spouse and kids, extended family, close friends, small groups at church, or neighbors. There might be transactions that take place, but mostly the purpose of your conversations will be to make your relationship stronger.

Most people will be somewhere in the middle, such as your boss, clients, physician, or casual friends. You're probably doing some transactional things with them, but there's also some level of relationship since you see them pretty often.

Deciding where someone is on the continuum will help you determine your purpose as you approach conversations with them. The clearer that purpose is, the more courage you'll have to say what needs to be said, and the more likely that you won't say things you later regret.

Conversational Outcomes

Outcomes are critical in most areas of life. Whether it's a vacation, a career path, or retirement goals, you need to know your destination. Otherwise, you're just on a road trip where your only purpose is to drive. If your destination is worth visiting, it's worth planning the trip.

We plan vacations carefully because we want the outcome of everyone having a good time together. We plan to move to a new house because we want the outcome of adequate space and a better layout for our growing family. We plan for the purchase of a new car because we want the outcome of how we'll feel when we're driving it.

This is just as true with conversations, though most people don't think about it. Our relationships are the most critical part of our lives, but we usually don't put any time into planning the outcome. We figure that conversations just happen. Either they go well or they don't. It's not something we plan for, because we can't predict what will happen.

We've all had a lot of experience with freezing up when we need to speak up but don't have the courage to do so—or with speaking up in the moment only to say something we later regret. Our main purpose is to avoid both of those situations. To do that, we need to plan for our desired outcome.

What does planning look like in conversations?

The place to start any important conversation is before it occurs. That's when you decide what you want the outcome to be. This is more than just thinking, *I hope this conversation goes well.* It's deciding what you'd like to see happen as the result of your time talking together.

Do you want to feel closer to the other person?

Do you want to understand them better?

Do you want them to understand you?

Do you want them to know some key information or facts?

Do you want to brainstorm a list of ideas on a subject?

Do you want to be more connected?

Do you want to build trust?

Do you need to make a decision?

Are you just looking for fun?

This doesn't take a lot of thought or pondering. It's usually something you can do easily before a conversation starts, simply by asking yourself what your desired outcome is. You're not taking spontaneity out of the conversation; you're just giving yourself a clear sense of what you want to achieve.

That doesn't mean *every* conversation has to have a goal. It's more critical when the stakes are high, the relationship is important, or the outcome is uncertain. As with any worthwhile goal, having a clear focus on what you want changes the way you communicate.

It's kind of like taking that family vacation by driving from Los Angeles to New York City. You've never been there, so your goal is to be in New York and enjoy the city together. How will you know when you've reached your destination? You'll see the Empire State Building.

Once you know your destination, you plan how to get there. You pull up a map program on your computer to determine your options, since there are a number of different routes to New York. You might want to take the quickest route. Maybe you're not in a hurry and would like to take a scenic route. Or maybe you want to avoid deserts or mountain routes, or go through states you've never been through. Maybe you want to walk or bike sometimes. In each case, the map helps you decide between your alternatives.

With that information, you're ready to start the trip. You get in the car and start driving—but find out that the road is closed ahead. Do you turn around and go back home? No; you (or your GPS) look for an alternate route. Which one? Whichever one will take you to New York. That's the outcome you're going for, so it impacts every decision you make along the way.

That's what happens in conversations when you're clear on the outcome. The conversation will take unexpected twists and turns, and you're not sure how to respond. But you won't have to stop talking and go home. You'll simply look for a solution that keeps you moving toward your destination. Know what you want from a conversation, then aim for it.

If you've ever wondered why you're feeling frustrated at how some conversations turn out, it might be because you're on a verbal road trip. You're being casual about the conversation instead of intentional, which would explain why you're never sure how you got where you ended up.

Tips for Transactional Conversations

When you're going to have a conversation with someone on the transactional side of the scale, take time to think through exactly what you want and need. Don't just focus on the details, because it's easy to end up getting caught in the weeds of trivial concerns. What's the outcome you're looking for?

- If you're looking for a car, prioritize what's important to you:
  - How important is dependability?
  - How important are mileage, size, and appearance?
  - What will you be using it for?
  - How much are you willing to pay?
  - If you buy a pickup truck, will all of your friends suddenly need help moving?
  - Why do you need this car? What will it enable you to do that you can't do now?
- The last question is the most important. You're not buying a car just to have a car but for what having it will accomplish. That's the purpose—the ¾-inch hole instead of the ¾-inch drill bit.
- It might be helpful to write down your answers so you have them to refer to when you're under pressure. When your purpose is crystal clear and you've determined the outcome, it is easier to negotiate. The salesperson might make suggestions that sound feasible, but you can always measure them against your desired outcome: *Will that give us what we ultimately need a car for, or is it a distraction?*

In any transaction, deciding what you need simplifies the conversation and how you participate.

Tips for Relational Conversations

Relational conversations are usually with people who will be there for the long haul. They stick around, so it's worth the effort to maintain those relationships and keep them healthy. It's a long-term commitment, so we make our biggest investment in their well-being. In each conversation, we consider how we can add value.

Here are five principles of long-term commitment:

1. **We take better care of things when we plan on keeping them.** When we have a long-haul mindset in a relationship, we'll spend the necessary time to keep it healthy. We know that if we take that relationship for granted, we're risking the long-term outcome.

2. **Relationships need regular maintenance.** No matter how well I wash my car, it will get dirty again once it sits outside for a few days. It never gets cleaner by itself. Keeping our best relationships "clean" takes intentional effort and regular attention. When we notice unhealthy words or attitudes creeping in, they should be graciously acknowledged and dealt with as early as possible.

3. **Relationships need to be protected.** Pollution, bird droppings, and tree sap take much longer to destroy a car's paint if it's protected by a good coat of wax. Without the wax, they begin to eat into the finish and ruin it. Strengthening and protecting a relationship needs to happen regularly before the bird droppings hit.

4. **It's easier to do routine maintenance than repairs.** It takes time and energy to maintain our most important relationships, but not as much as fixing things that go wrong. Consistently invest in your best relationships, and the chance for success grows exponentially.

5. **Without intentional effort, relationships deteriorate.** The second law of thermodynamics says that, left on their own, things tend to run down—not up. When we take our key relationships for granted because there's no big or obvious problem, decay begins to attack quietly. We only notice when the relationship becomes painful.

Patterns of Purpose

Knowing where you're headed in every conversation doesn't take a lot of time or effort, just some careful thinking ahead of time. It's something that almost no one does, but the payoff can be huge.

Want your conversations to make a difference? Know where you're going!

13

Being Humble
without Being Weak

*What the world needs is more geniuses with humility;
there are so few of us left.*

Oscar Levant

When we're meeting someone for the first time, we usually say, "Hi! How are you?" The typical response is, "Fine. How are you?" It doesn't mean a whole lot and is more of a conversation starter to get things moving, kind of like striking a match to light a campfire. You can't cook s'mores with that first little spark, but it has the potential to start a blaze.

Have you ever asked someone "How are you?" and they proceed to tell you about how bad traffic was, the irritating person they ran into at a restaurant, and how much better things would be if certain politicians weren't in office? It feels like they tossed a cup of gasoline on your question and things erupted. You're thinking, *Whoa, I didn't* really *want to know how you were. I was just being polite.*

In the early stages of any conversation, we're trying to get a sense of who the other person is. We look for common ground to discuss and start sharing our ideas and perspectives with each other. Subconsciously, we're sizing the other person up to decide what we think of them. We're listening to their tone of voice, watching their expressions and body language, taking in their words, and looking for hints about who they are.

If they seem open and genuine, we tend to like them. If they seem artificial and arrogant, we tend to dislike them. Right or wrong, we form an opinion pretty quickly—and once we've decided, it's hard to change our minds.

At the same time, we know they're sizing us up in the same way. Without even realizing it, we're crafting the image we're presenting so they'll see us in the best light. We aren't going to tell them all of our failures and fears and insecurities because they might not like us. We don't want to appear weak, so we act confident to make a good impression whether we're feeling confident or not.

As author Mel Schwartz says, "Acting strong is still acting." He continues, "When we act or pretend to be different than who we really are, we abandon our real self . . . in an attempt to control what we hope others will think of us."[1] He suggests that if our self-esteem comes from what others think of us, it's actually "other-esteem." It comes from others, not from ourselves.

When we're evaluating others, we're attracted to them if they're genuine, real, and unpretentious. When we feel like they're not being real, we're not interested in pursuing the relationship. Even if they don't say anything, we just sense that they're counterfeit rather than the real thing. Why would we bother to build a genuine relationship with a counterfeit person?

Being real is a strength, and it draws people to you. Hiding your true self is weakness, and it causes people to resist connecting with you.

The connecting point is *humility*.

156

Pretending to Be Humble

I met with someone who had been a human resources director for most of his career, interviewing and selecting people for open positions at the company. He told me he'd probably conducted several thousand interviews over the years and had become good at reading between the lines of a prospective employee's answers.

"What's the biggest thing you've seen that keeps people from getting selected?" I asked. I assumed it would be a lack of experience, not preparing properly for the interview, or even the way they dressed.

"Humblebragging," he said. "I ask them to tell me one of their biggest weaknesses, and they say, 'I'm always working too hard for everyone else' or 'It's hard for me to work on a team because I'm such a perfectionist.' They are using false humility to convince me how qualified they are, and I know they're not being real or vulnerable. It screams 'dishonest' and ensures I won't hire them."

Most of us understand that genuine humility and openness are attractive to others. If we're feeling insecure, that can start a downward spiral.

1. We don't feel self-confident, so we think we have to appear perfect.
2. However, we know perfect people don't seem human, so others don't like them.
3. We know humility is attractive, so we pretend to be humble.
4. People typically respond in one of two ways: either they put us on a pedestal and can't relate to us, or they can sense we're just pretending.

True humility is tough. People who are humble usually don't realize it. Anytime you start to notice you're humble, it's easy to take pride in that. It's like the old country song by Mac Davis: "Oh Lord it's hard to be humble when you're perfect in every way."[2]

We're tempted to think it takes aggressiveness to get ahead. Humility sounds like the exact opposite, like playing tackle football with a pillow taped across your shoulders instead of real pads. In reality, humility is what you get when you quit seeing yourself as better than or less than others. It sees everyone as valuable because of who they are—including you.

It's called being *human*—and it's something everyone on the planet shares. We're all on different journeys, and we're trying to find our way. When we compare our journey with someone else's, it's easy to think our journey is better or worse than theirs. It means we're trying to go on someone else's journey, which is futile.

If you're building your self-worth on the opinions of others, you want them to see you as strong—and humility feels wimpy. You feel "less than." It's only when you've built confidence around your own uniqueness that humility becomes a strength. When you're secure internally, you don't feel a need to impress others. You won't have to brag about your accomplishments because they're not the basis for who you are. True humility is a by-product of true confidence, which comes from getting your self-worth from the right place.

When you have genuine confidence, you have the tools to speak up in conversations where you might normally hold back. You won't worry about how others respond, because it's not threatening. At the same time, humility lets you focus on others and their needs more than yourself, so you'll know how to temper your words to keep from offending others. You'll be able to catch yourself before saying the wrong thing because you're sensitive to what's appropriate in any conversation.

Ten Traits of Genuine Humility

It's easier to be humble when you're new at something. Your first day on the job, you don't know much and have no delusions of expertise. When you bring your first baby home from the hospital, you realize you don't know what you're doing and there's no instruction manual. In these cases, humility is the recognition of reality, knowing you don't have any tools in your toolbox.

Over time, your skills grow. You learn what it takes to do your job, and you pick up the tools you need by trying things out. With the baby, you vow to give half of your income to charity if your child—and you—could sleep through just one night.

In most cases, you get pretty good at your roles the longer you're in them. By the time you become a senior executive, your toolbox is loaded—and you know you're good at what you do. Once your kids make it through their teenage years, you might feel good about your parenting skills and realize that their choices are their own, not a reflection on you.

Humility means you know you're good at what you do, but that doesn't make you better than others who are first starting out. Pride is when you want others to be impressed with you because of what you've learned or the skills you have. Humility is knowing those things are true but having the confidence to connect with anyone at a human level. You don't minimize your skills but accept their reality. As it is commonly said, humility is "not to think less of yourself, but to think of yourself less."

So, what are the characteristics of a person with true humility—and how can we build those characteristics into our own lives? Use these ten traits of humble people to evaluate your own humility.

1. They're Aware of What's Happening around Them

Confident, humble people aren't positioning themselves to be noticed. Instead, they're keenly aware of the dynamics of every situation. That includes their own feelings, as well as what's happening between other people. They naturally watch all of those dynamics to develop a mental map of the entire situation. They see the big picture instead of just the moving pieces and are focused outward on others rather than inward on their own self-esteem.

2. They Care about Others

When someone is humble, they think of others more than themselves. They're not always wondering how others are viewing them because they're secure in their self-worth. Since they're not looking for affirmation, they're free to invest in those around them. Their confidence allows them to help others grow and "get better" by encouraging them and meeting their needs. They find practical ways to build up the people they encounter, helping them have the mental strength to face the challenges of life.

Even the Bible reinforces this idea: "Don't be jealous or proud, but be humble and consider others more important than yourselves. Care about them as much as you care about yourselves" (Phil. 2:3–4).

3. They're Good Listeners

Humble people are more interested in learning about the other person's perspective than impressing them with their own thoughts. They truly want to know what the other person thinks because they care about that person. They treat the other person with respect when they listen, because it shows they value their thoughts.

4. They Admit When They're Wrong

Insecure people can't risk being wrong, so they defend themselves and blame others. Unfortunately, people can almost always see through the charade and lose respect. A person with genuine confidence isn't dependent on perfection and has a keen sense of their own humanity. When they make a mistake, they don't make excuses. They simply say, "I was wrong."

A person who can admit they're wrong builds trust with others because they're being honest. It's not always comfortable, but it's always powerful.

5. They Always Want to Learn More

Some people believe whatever opinions they have are accurate, so there's no need for more information. Other people believe they're right but are always looking at different perspectives to grow and complete their paradigm. They're humble enough to know they don't know everything about anything, so they have a drive to learn as much as possible, and they're willing to release or expand their positions based on the new information. They're curious and want to learn from the experience of others.

6. They're Grateful

No one makes it to the top without the help of others. Prideful people get there and think, *Look at what I've accomplished.* Humble people recognize the reality of the accomplishment but are never afraid to express gratitude to everyone they encounter.

It's the company CEO who drops into the mailroom to thank a line worker for their contribution.

It's the successful person who writes a note to one of their high school teachers to let them know how much they appreciate their input in their life.

It's the restaurant patron who leaves a generous tip and a note that reads, "Thanks for brightening our day."

They have what author Zig Ziglar called an "attitude of gratitude," and it has become their way of life.

7. They Want Everyone to "Win"

Confident people with humility have a drive to succeed. They want to win, but never at the expense of others. Whenever they're negotiating, they want an outcome that meets both their own needs and those of the other person. They don't believe in "winners" and "losers" but work hard to find mutually beneficial solutions. If they can't find a solution that achieves that end, they're often willing to back out of a deal where they could easily be the winner—if the other person can't win too.

Winning can be a weak solution if others are hurt in the process, so it takes strength to help others get what they need as well.

8. They're Proactive

Proactivity means taking personal responsibility for one's choices. There is never finger-pointing or blame, because a humble person owns their decisions. If the decision doesn't turn out well, they take responsibility and apologize when needed. "I'm sorry" is never a sign of weakness, and only people with inner confidence are able to use those two words with integrity.

The best leaders own their words, actions, and choices, including the consequences. If a project turns out well, they tell others, "With your help, we did this together." If it turns out poorly, they say, "This was my choice, and it didn't turn out well. I own this, and I'm sorry."

9. They're Outwardly Focused

People who lack self-confidence are always focused inward—wondering how they're coming across to others and how they're being perceived. Confident people don't need that because they have internal security. That frees them to focus consistently on the lives of the people around them.

It's as though they see a sign around everyone's neck that reads, "Make my life better today." It's their mission to encourage every person they meet so they'll have the vision to move forward in their lives. Generosity of attention is the hallmark of a humble person who wants to make a dent in the world.

10. They're Willing to Ask for Help

When someone is humble, they realize they don't know everything—and they don't have to. They know the value others bring and freely tap into their contributions. They know what they know and what they don't know, and they're quick to trust others to fill the gaps. When they ask others for help, they know those people become "better" because they're being valued for their contribution.

First Steps

Humility might sound negative if you don't think you have anything to offer. Or you might be struggling with pride because of your success and haven't considered the life-giving power of true humility. Where can you start?

Look over the ten characteristics above and pick one you'd like to explore. Write it down, then brainstorm ideas about what you can do to begin testing it out. Go for tiny steps, not perfection. When you find success in small actions, you'll gain confidence to try bigger steps. Over time, you'll grow into the process and gain confidence in how you impact others.

Humility isn't weakness; it can become your greatest strength in conversations and relationships.

Try it on for size. I promise it will look good on you!

PART 3

Inside-Out Communication

When I first started writing this book, I went to the bookstore to see what other books had been written on this topic. I did a similar search online and purchased a number of titles. My goal was to see what was already out there so I could write something different.

Most of them focused on how to be more assertive in conversation, to speak up when it was hard. They included scripting to use in various situations: "When this happens, try saying this." It was great advice, much like the suggestions I've seen in a lot of self-help books. I've read many of those books over the years and identified with the examples. I would think back to a time when I was in a similar situation and thought, *I wish I'd had that response when I needed it.*

So I'd buy the book, hoping it would help me in future situations. But I usually found its advice easier to apply to past encounters than future ones. It always felt like I'd have to memorize hundreds of different responses to be able to have just the right one ready when I needed it. When the future encounter happened, I could never remember which response to use. I'd feel like saying, "Hold on a second—I need to check this book to find something to say to you."

Even if I remembered what to say, the other person never responded the way the script in the book worked. I might have said something well, but it didn't automatically bring agreement. When we're dealing with real people, we still have to negotiate the relationship and emotions, not just have clever responses.

I discovered what was missing for me. All the other books focused on things you could *say*, not who you *were*. Courageous conversation doesn't come from saying courageous things; it comes from becoming a courageous person.

Who you are on the inside determines how you come across on the outside. You don't have to pretend to be courageous; you can become confident in who you are, capitalizing on your uniqueness.

That's the journey we've been on, and it's the focus for this last section. What happens when you become the best possible version of yourself? You find the confidence to be real, which launches you on a journey of impact. You'll be able to speak up when needed with courageous words that are laced with compassion, and you won't have to memorize anything.

You'll be able to confront with grace because you care deeply. It's not about just feeling stronger in your conversational skills; it's about communicating with compassion and kindness. The need to be abrasive or sarcastic disappears.

It's an inside-out job.

14

How to Speak Up for Others

It's easy to stand in the crowd, but it takes
courage to stand alone.

Gandhi

Aaron rode with his new boss to an important client meeting across town. When they arrived, the parking lot was full—and they were running late. After a few minutes, his boss pulled into a disabled-person parking space near the entrance. There were dozens of people walking by, so the boss faked a limp until he was inside the building. Aaron hated it when people without a disability parked in those spaces but didn't know how to confront his boss for fear of retribution. So he kept quiet.

What would you have done?

Most of us believe we would have the courage to speak up when it's needed, but we often freeze at the last second. We have great intentions, but there are a number of things that keep us from speaking out:

- We're afraid of what someone else will think about us or say to us.

167

- Tough conversations are uncomfortable.
- We're afraid we'll damage a relationship.
- If our self-esteem comes from the opinions of others, we can't risk their disapproval.
- We assume somebody else will speak up and we won't have to.
- We just don't want to get involved.

But if we don't speak up, we allow the injustice to continue—which harms us and others. Sometimes a person is a victim of someone's verbal or emotional abuse, but they don't have the internal resources to defend themselves. We don't want to intervene or get involved, so we remain silent. And the abuse continues.

What if you're part of a work group discussing a situation that needs a solution? Most people are moving enthusiastically toward a plan that you see as unfair to older group members. You don't want to be seen as negative, and it's easiest to simply stay quiet. But if you don't speak your mind, your silence implies you agree—and the unfairness would not be addressed.

When is it appropriate to speak up for others? Why is it so hard to do so? How and when should we do it?

Could You Be a Whistleblower?

When we recognize there could be real consequences to speaking up, it can make it tough to take action. We want to stand up against wrong, but we think of what could happen and ask ourselves, *Is it worth it?*

In some situations, the consequences might simply be uncomfortable:

- You want to tell a server your meal is overcooked or they got your order wrong.

- You are being ignored at a checkout counter as several cashiers are focused on their own conversation.
- You are forced to listen to the person at the table next to you at the restaurant talking loudly on their phone.

But what about when the risk is much greater, where there's a chance of losing your job or a relationship if you speak up? If you point out an injustice, someone might have the power to make your life miserable as a result. What then?

Decades ago, factory workers depended on their jobs for survival. Management could mistreat them, hold back their pay, or engage in dishonest practices that could impact an entire community—but they knew no one would complain. Anyone who spoke up was called a "whistleblower" and was immediately punished.

A whistleblower is a person who sees something wrong and reports it. It's almost always in a situation where there could be consequences for saying something, especially in a business or government setting. For example, if a person has evidence leaders in their organization are doing things that are illegal, unethical, or dangerous, it would make sense that they would report it. They might hesitate for a number of reasons:

- They're afraid of losing their job.
- They won't be fired, but they know those leaders could make their lives miserable or block their career path.
- They might look foolish.
- Saying something could make things worse for others.
- They'll get blamed if others lose their jobs because they exposed the issue.
- They're afraid they'll have to testify or share in a public setting, and they get intimidated when people ask pointed questions.

To prevent these things, whistleblower protection laws were put into effect in the late 1980s. These laws allow people to anonymously speak up about what they've observed without having to worry about repercussions. They have to present a lot of evidence to prove their claim, which keeps them from randomly making accusations, but they don't have to reveal their identity. This provides a way for people to speak up without having to have a confrontation.

The same principle applies in our personal relationships. Someone can act in a way that is harmful or dishonest, and they damage relationships in the process. We see it happening, and we want to speak up in protest. But the repercussions are much more personal and impactful; we can't do it anonymously and there are no "personal whistleblower" laws in place to protect us and the people we care about.

How did you feel when you read that paragraph? See if any of these apply:

- You feel guilty because you don't speak up for others when you think you should.
- You hear or see things that make you think, *Wait—that's not right.*
- Other people seem to be much more articulate, and it takes you longer to process your thoughts, so you feel inadequate to jump in with your perspective.
- There are so many wrong things happening that you feel overwhelmed.
- You're only one person and the issues are big, so you feel like your voice won't make a difference.
- You want to say something, but fear rejection and repercussion.
- You haven't clearly thought through your position, so you feel like you can't say anything until you're confident of your perspective.

Those are legitimate concerns, and the solution is not as simple as saying, "Just have more courage and do it anyway." That's like being hurt in a car accident and having someone tell you, "Just stop bleeding." There are bigger issues that need to be addressed before we're able to speak up the way we want and need to. Otherwise, we risk low-impact babbling instead of laser-focused precision.

The good news is you have a voice, and you have something to say. The even better news is you have the ability to use that voice; it's a skill that can be crafted and learned. The key is your approach; it has to come out of your own uniqueness and temperament.

Nobody does *you* better than you.

Playing the Cello in a Marching Band

One of the reasons we feel inadequate is our perception of what it means to speak up for others. We see vocal people make an impact, and we assume we need to do what they're doing. If people are protesting, we think the logical thing to do is to join the protest. If others are debating an issue on social media, we think we need to chime in with our thoughts. If some family members get angry with another family member's repeated actions, we think we need to express our anger in the same way.

The problem is if we only add our voice to those of the crowd, it becomes diluted, like adding a drop of water to the ocean. We can feel pressure to participate when people say, "Join us. We need your support because the more of us there are, the more impact we'll have." There's some truth in that, because bigger things are harder to ignore.

But we're talking about you, personally, making a difference that's unique. You can make an impact no one else is capable of, and you don't have to change your basic temperament to do so. Running for office, speaking up at a city council

171

meeting, or joining a protest might not be how you're wired, even though these are often the first things people who want to make a difference think of. Your unique temperament is the foundation for your impact, and it makes it easier to make a genuine difference.

Late speaker and author Jim Rohn said, "Success lies in the opposite direction of the normal pull."[1] When we join the crowd and do what they're doing, our uniqueness jumps in the back seat, and our most valuable contribution may be marginalized. It's like being a cellist but joining the marching band: people might notice, but only because you seem out of place. Impact comes when you embrace your uniqueness, doing and saying what nobody else is doing or saying—because nobody else is you.

In the film *The Legend of Bagger Vance*, Will Smith plays a golf caddy who speaks like a philosopher. In one scene he says, "Inside each and every one of us is our one, true authentic swing. Something we was born with. Something that's ours and ours alone. Something that can't be learned. Something that's gotta be remembered."[2]

Find your swing, and you'll find your voice.

That might seem terrifying, because it sounds like you have to become loud and noisy to stand up for something or someone. It's tough enough to speak up for your own ideas, and sometimes even tougher to speak up for someone else. For a lot of us, it's just easier to stay silent and let everybody else sort through the issues. But when you're silent, people assume you're agreeing with the crowd. When your voice is absent from the discussion, you end up with counterfeit group consensus.

Where Do We Start?

We can see a host of injustices in society that need attention. There are humanitarian issues around the world, moral and spiritual issues that demand intervention, and philosophical and political positions that deserve attention. Closer to home, we have things happening in our workplaces that cause deep frustration, church concerns that cause division, and family members making choices that cause pain. All of those issues cry out for attention, and the ones that touch us directly tug at our hearts to jump in.

Those issues are real, and most seem vitally important. We're moved by many of them and want to use our voice. But we only have so much bandwidth and energy; the more issues we focus on, the more we dilute our impact and multiply our frustration. The narrower we can focus, the more impact we'll have.

That means we have to pick our battles. It's tough to fix the world, but we can make a difference where we have influence. The first step is to accept our limitations as humans, so we should determine which issues we're going to leave to someone else. Those other concerns can still touch our hearts but not claim our energy and attention. That allows us to choose issues where we can speak up for others and make something happen. As the old Chinese proverb says, "He who chases two rabbits catches neither."

Another factor is how much the issue impacts you personally. It's great to stand up for large causes like homelessness or prison reform. But if you know someone personally who needs your voice to represent them, it's a chance to pinpoint your efforts for that individual.

Personal challenges deserve a solid helping of your focus, because they impact your world more than public challenges. Otherwise, you risk being the plumber who helps everyone else but has leaky pipes at home.

Using your voice doesn't have to always be in-person, loudly, in public. For you, your voice might be the most powerful when you use it in writing—sending letters or writing opinion pieces or even articles to raise awareness. Speaking in public might reach the few dozen people in the room, while a magazine article could be read by millions. The key is that your voice has to be *yours*, used in a way that lets you express yourself powerfully as you represent issues for those who can't use their own voice. Who does that include?

- People who can't adequately speak for themselves, such as children being bullied, abused, or treated unfairly (including your own); elderly and disabled people with medical issues they can't fight for (but probably understand better than their doctors), and those who have been marginalized.
- Someone in a tough situation who doesn't have the resources to find a solution.
- Someone in a group setting who isn't being included in a discussion, especially when their perspective isn't being valued in an attempt to reach consensus.
- People in situations where the stakes are high, such as family members who can't advocate for themselves though the issue impacts the entire family.
- Anyone who is being ignored, and you have the ability to draw the right kind of attention to them.

When you have a combination of passion and platform, you're the perfect person to step up and intervene.

Giving Others a Voice

Once you've identified who you should represent, how do you make it happen? Since you're building your own method based on your own situation and uniqueness, there's no exact science. But here are some considerations to factor into the process.

Write

If you're more gifted in written communication than verbal, consider crafting your words in a powerful way to be used in an appropriate setting. Often this will be an email or document to a person who can make a difference, and you become the one who makes the connection. This isn't about writing because you don't have the courage to speak; it's about using your strongest gifts to make a difference.

Listen

Resist the temptation to jump in and speak for someone before you talk to them. Don't assume you know what they need; take the time to sit with them and ask them. Otherwise, you might end up with a solution that doesn't meet the real need (remember the tractors in Ethiopia).

Draw Attention to Them, Not You

When you feel the need to speak up for others, draw attention to them—not yourself. It's tempting to get people to focus on you as the advocate, but you end up stealing their voice. Make it about them, and step back.

Give Them Tools

As the old proverb says, "Give a man a fish, and you feed him for a day. Teach him how to fish, and you feed him for a lifetime." That means you're not just fixing the issue temporarily but helping them develop the skills needed to speak for themselves. Talk to them and get their perspective, so the skills developed are appropriate for the situation.

Talk to Them, Not about Them

An elderly woman is lying in her hospital bed while her doctors and family members are discussing her condition and decisions that need to be made. "Excuse me," she says firmly. "I'm right here, and I'm not deaf. This is my body you're talking about, so don't ignore me. Talk to me." It's a matter of dignity and respect. You want to be a person's voice (with their permission) to the degree that they can't speak for themselves, but let them use whatever voice they have. You're adding to their voice, not replacing it.

Speak, but Don't Force

Your role is to represent the needs of another person as accurately as possible. That means speaking up in a way that demonstrates respect. You can advocate with firmness, but don't become belligerent. You want your speech to attract the right people, not repel them.

Stay in Your Strength

What's your greatest skill in communicating with others? That's how you should speak up. If you're not quick on your feet with answers, don't get involved in debate. Ask questions, actively listen to the responses, and then craft your response in the form of follow-up questions for the next conversation. The more you can be yourself, the less intimidated you'll feel in conversations.

You don't have to have perfect answers; rather, try to have perfect questions that help you understand the other person's perspective. Building trust comes through listening and understanding, which opens the door for mutual solutions.

Be Open to Change

In an earlier chapter, we talked about how two people can believe they're "right" because they're both looking at an issue through their own filters—the back of the house versus the front of the house. That leads to a battle of "who's right," with no progress being made.

Listen and question carefully to see through the other person's lenses—not to replace your position but to clarify it. Then invite the other person to do the same. It softens the relationship and builds trust when you work together toward a solution rather than seeing who "wins." Someone can be strong but still be wrong; how do you know it's not you?

Focus on Outcomes

When you're speaking up for someone else, have a crystal-clear picture in mind of exactly what outcome you're looking for. That keeps the discussion from taking side roads and focusing on less important issues. Try to come to an agreement about what the desired outcome is, so everyone involved stays focused on what matters most.

Make It a Lifestyle

You don't need a huge platform or a big name before you can speak up for others who can't. It's common for people to feel like there's nothing they can do because the needs are so many and so big. They give up because they don't feel like anyone would listen to them either.

You have your own unique voice, and it's your superpower. You have the ability, in your own way, to speak up for others. Don't wait until you've built the courage to feel comfortable in every situation. Begin to make it a part of your daily routine. When you notice something, take a tiny step of courage.

For example, you're in a meeting at work where most of the group is vocal and energized around a project they're considering. You know one person in the group—let's call her Sarah—is quiet and rarely speaks up on her own. But you also know she's a deep-thinking introvert and usually has some of the best ideas to contribute. Take the simple step of saying, "You know, before we decide, I think Sarah has had some experience in this type of thing. I'd love to get her input before we land on a solution."

You didn't speak *for* her but rather did what was appropriate for you to make an opportunity for her voice to be heard.

Pay attention each day to what you see around you. Notice the things that catch your attention and make you think, *Wait—that's not right*. Instead of feeling guilty for not doing anything, ask yourself, *Is there some little thing I could do to make a difference?*

Start small, and your courage will grow over time. You can become the person who speaks up for others when it's needed.

That's how one person can change the world.

15

Getting Feedback

Take my advice; I'm not using it.

Anonymous

If people could do a customer review on you, how many stars would you get?

People use online review apps such as Yelp to see what other people think about restaurants and services. If the reviews are good, they might consider using that service. If the reviews are bad, they avoid it.

We all have our "default" restaurant—the one we keep going to whenever we can't decide where else to go. It's familiar, it's comfortable, and it's safe. Maybe they don't have the greatest food in the world, but it's pretty consistent. Some days the food might be a little off or the service a little shaky. But we know the place well enough to realize that it's just a bad day for them, and it'll be better next time.

But if someone makes a first-time visit on that bad day, they might be incensed. They demand free food, won't pay the bill, and write a scathing review online as soon as they can. They want to punish the restaurant and protect others from the same fate.

What if there were a "people" category on Yelp, where people could critique family members and friends? What would they write? Would it reflect the realities of long-term commitment, or would it be an impulsive reaction to their last frustrating conversation?

> I've been a regular for a number of years with John. In those early years, he met all my expectations of a husband. But my recent experiences have caused me to lower my ratings because his customer service seems to have disappeared. I married him because he was the strong, silent type; now he never talks to me. I admired his strong convictions about the things that bugged him in society; now he just complains about the things that bug him about me. Unfortunately, I can no longer recommend him as a husband.

> You would think that after three years, a person would learn from their mistakes and correct them. But Tommy still seems more committed to his own interests than the welfare of others. His performance as a toddler is steadily declining, his social skills have become consistently self-centered, and he has little commitment to our family structure. It's sad to watch 5-star potential disintegrate to a 2-star review. We'll keep him for now, but we're disappointed.

> Uncle Joe? He's crazy. But we made it through the last holiday without him causing a scene. That's a miracle, and it might have been a fluke. But it's enough to add a couple of stars to his rating.

We all want people to like us. It's human nature to want five-star reviews, and we feel great when they happen. If we get a one-star review, it hurts. That's why we tend to seek out positive feedback and try to protect ourselves from negative feedback. Unfortunately, that means we're not trying to hear the truth so we can grow and improve; we're simply looking for people to reinforce the good things we do so we can feel better about ourselves.

This is one of the key tactics of people pleasers: trying to make everyone else happy so we'll be seen positively, crafting our image to protect ourselves from hurt.

Can You Handle Honest Feedback?

Researcher and author Dr. Carol Dweck describes two primary paradigms that people use in going through life: a *fixed mindset* and a *growth mindset*.[1] They're two different lenses we use to decide how we'll negotiate life.

People with a *fixed mindset* believe they were born with a certain amount of intelligence, so they spend their lives proving themselves. They want to be seen as successful and smart and want to be accepted rather than rejected. That's why they avoid tough challenges and give up when things get hard. They see negative feedback as threatening, so they ignore it as much as possible.

People with a *growth mindset* believe they can always become better and keep learning, so challenges become stepping-stones to success instead of barricades. When things get tough, they keep going instead of giving up. Negative feedback is seen as a chance to get better, and they actively seek it out.

Feedback is essential for growth. It's not always comfortable, but it's the quickest way to find out how you're doing. It's the equivalent of looking in the mirror midway through a social event and finding out that you have broccoli between your teeth. It's embarrassing, but you're grateful you discovered it when you did.

Last week, I had the chance to speak virtually to a small group of executives. I've done thousands of live presentations but had not done very many virtual ones until the pandemic started. It went well, I thought, and the CEO was more than pleased with how the presentation connected with his people. He sent me the video so I could have it for my files.

When I watched it, I noticed that my computer screen was reflecting in my glasses most of the time. I'm a stickler about eye contact when I'm speaking because it's the key to connecting with any audience. In this case, they couldn't even see my eyes.

My first reaction was that it ruined the presentation, but it hadn't. People might have noticed, but they were more interested in the content. I wish it hadn't happened, but I was grateful to have had that opportunity to grow. In the future, I'll take steps to avoid it—and I'll be a better virtual presenter as a result.

People with a growth mindset don't enjoy negative feedback, but they seek it out. They know that it gets easier over time if they pursue it often, so they find ways to make it safe for others to let them know what's really happening.

Managers have heard that there's value in feedback, so they ask their employees to chime in with their thoughts. Often, no one says anything, or they just say, "No, everything's OK." It might not be the truth. The truth may be that they don't feel safe enough to speak up. What does that lack of safety look like?

- The manager responds with defensiveness or excuses whenever something negative is shared.
- Employees are afraid there will be repercussions if they tell the truth.
- The manager always has to be in control, and the employees don't have a voice in anything that happens.
- There's no trust in the relationship.
- The manager has a fixed mindset.

In any setting, most people are uncomfortable giving feedback because they don't want to hurt anyone's feelings. They usually don't resort to lying, but they'll do their best to avoid sharing the truth. Fortunately, there's a process to follow when asking for feedback that makes it safe for people to respond.

How to Get to the Truth

As I'm writing this, I realize there's something I need to do.

I have an executive leader at our company who is over a large region that I'm a part of. She's not my boss, but I'm part of her team in a broad sense. I've worked with her for years and we know each other well, and it's a safe relationship with a great deal of trust that's been built.

I've gotten plenty of positive feedback from her over the years, as well as others I work with on her team, but I realize I've never asked her for negative feedback. I know it's safe, and she'd tell me the truth. It would be an opportunity to get priceless input that could make a big difference in my career and impact.

But I don't want to. I like hearing the good stuff because it feels good. At the same time, it's easy to get addicted to the good stuff and avoid the stuff that's good for me—kind of like eating ice cream and avoiding kale.

So, I'm going to take a short break from writing and send her an email. Here's what it will say:

> I have a favor to ask. I know we've worked together for a long time, and I believe we have a high-trust relationship. You also lead the team of people that I interact with the most. I generally get good feedback from them (and you), but not the negative stuff . . . things that could help me grow. Either there isn't any negative, or they're just not telling me.
>
> You have a better handle on what your people are thinking because you work with them every day (and hear them whining). I want to grow and get better. Based on your perspective and experience, what do I need to know—the blind spots—that could help me become more impactful and effective?

I value your thoughts. I don't want to hear the negative stuff any more than I want to hear that I have malaria. But there's no growth without knowledge.

They say "ignorance is bliss." I don't want to be that happy . . .

OK, that email is on its way. I think I'm sweating just a little. Hopefully by the end of this chapter, I'll be able to let you know how it turned out.

Back to business. We've been talking about the value of feedback in general. It's something that can change your life, just like getting regular physical exams. Now, let's narrow it down to the topic of this book: communication. How can we find out what our blind spots are when we're in conversation? High-stakes conversations can be challenging and uncomfortable, and we're on "high alert" to negotiate the dynamics.

In most conversations, we usually aren't paying attention to how we're coming across. We're too busy sorting out our words, trying to say the right thing so we make our point. Other people probably notice how we come across, but they rarely tell us.

There's only one way to find out what they're thinking: *we have to ask*.

How can we provide an environment of safety where they're willing to share? There are two key components:

1. How we ask.
2. How we respond.

How to Ask for Feedback

If people don't tell us what they see in our communication patterns, we tend to think there aren't any problems. When you ask others for help, you're asking for a mirror to spot the broccoli.

You're not asking them for *advice*, which is more about their opinions of what you should do. You're looking for what they *observe*—what they see from their perspective.

Once you see what they see, you can determine what to do about it. That's your job, not theirs. Their job is simply to watch you with intentionality and give you feedback, both positive and negative.

To make it safe for them, consider these suggestions:

Prepare them ahead of time. Whether it's a corporate meeting, a presentation, or just being part of a family gathering, ask someone you trust if they would be willing to observe what happens in your communication throughout the event. If you ask ahead of time, it shifts them into "observation mode" so they can pay attention.

Be specific. Don't just ask them to observe; let them know exactly what you want to know about your style, your delivery, and how others respond. Instead of, "Let me know how I come across," ask, "Watch for things I say or do (body language, facial reactions, eye contact) when I'm talking to someone, and how they seem to respond." You'll get a much better response if you ask people to observe one or two things instead of just saying, "So, how did I do?"

Ask for the negative as well as the positive. Ask, "Are there things you observe that seem to stop people from interacting? What are my biggest strengths in communicating?"

Ask if they feel safe. It's a simple question, but it's important to know how free they feel to share honestly with you. Make it a choice for them to participate. Let them know that if they'd rather not do this, it's not a problem. You can easily ask someone else.

Schedule a debriefing. Find a time to meet, perhaps for coffee, a few days later. That gives them time to think through the best and most comfortable way to share their observations.

Use a scale of 1–10. When they first agree to help you, tell them you'd like to be rated using a scale of 1–10 on how effective you were as a communicator in the situation they observed. Then ask, "If I could work on one area that would raise that score by one point, what would it be?" You're not asking for advice, just blind spots.

How to Respond to Feedback

Safety comes from good experiences. People might be willing to give you feedback one time to see if it feels safe. If it goes well, they'll be more willing to share honestly in the future.

Keep these principles in mind as you respond to what they share:

Listen without any explanation. Getting defensive or making excuses for what they saw tells them you aren't really interested in their perspective. Listen deeply, and only ask questions for clarification. Prove that you just want to know exactly what they're seeing. If they say something vague or generic, ask for an example.

Take notes. Write down what they tell you. It shows you respect their words and value their perspective.

Thank them. It's risky for them to share at this level, so they're doing you a huge favor. When they're done, let them know how much you appreciate their thoughts, and that they have given you a lot to think about. A few days later, send them a note of gratitude for their time and care. They've given you a gift, so a thank-you note is appropriate.

Don't evaluate what they say. You might realize that their observation is somewhat biased by their own experiences or background. It's easy to dismiss what you hear when that happens, but keep an open mind for nuggets of truth.

Don't downplay the positive. If you find it hard to accept praise, remember that it's just as important as the negative. You just want to know their observations, no matter what they are. As you're processing what you hear, remember that the positive is just as real as the negative—so learn to accept all of it equally.

Time to Grow

Test the waters of feedback slowly if you're not used to it. It's like working out at a gym when you're out of shape. You want your initial experiences to be stretching but not overwhelming. The more you seek out feedback, the more it will become part of your toolkit for personal growth.

There's one simple way to give yourself feedback without anyone else being involved: find a way to make a video of your interactions with others. At a social event, prop up your phone off to one side and let the video run for five or ten minutes. You'll immediately see things you never knew were happening. Be careful, though, not to overevaluate yourself. We almost always focus on the negative and overlook the positive when watching ourselves. This could be a great time to involve your "observer" to make sure you're seeing yourself in a balanced way.

As author Ken Blanchard said, "Feedback is the breakfast of champions."[2] If you want a fast-track process for developing your communication skills, start getting an accurate picture of yourself.

Make feedback your best friend.

● ● ●

By the way . . . my executive friend told me she hasn't heard anything lately from anyone. That's a good sign, she said, because it implies that "no news is good news." She loved the fact that I reached out in order to grow and is going to talk to different people on her team. "If we find anything that needs attention," she said, "I will be sure to let you know in a meaningful and helpful way." So I'm not out of the woods yet—but I'm good, because we both understand the true value of feedback.

16

Why Change Can Be Your Best Friend

*If you don't like how things are, change it!
You're not a tree.*

Jim Rohn

My high school reunion was supposed to happen next month. It's a big one (another decade), and I've been looking forward to it since the last one ten years ago. But because of the pandemic, it's postponed indefinitely.

I'm bummed, disappointed, and sad. I wanted to be there because I've had to miss out on other reunions in the past. I saw the list of those planning to attend, and it includes people I would love to see again—casual friends, good friends, and best friends. There are some names on the list I can't remember, as well as a couple of girls I had a crush on (but never told them). We've lost a few friends over the years, and others seem to have vanished. I'm going to miss catching up and seeing where our journeys have taken us.

This change of plans got me thinking. What is it about a school reunion that impacts us so much? What makes us work so hard to lose weight, appear successful, and impress people we haven't seen for years? I've known people who skipped their reunion because they were embarrassed about their life.

When I think back to some of my friends, I remember them the way they were, not the way they are. They remember me the way I was too. Even though we know better, we picture them as being the same people they were when we were classmates.

Life takes us all in new directions. I'm not the same person I was in high school. Neither are my classmates. Neither are you. We've *changed*.

Change Is Constant

When it comes to friends we haven't seen in years, it doesn't take long to realize how much change there has been in every area of our lives. It's common sense that past people are different from present people. Life happens to all of us, and it carves the path we take throughout the years.

With these old friends, there are plenty of things to talk about because we get to explore their journey. We want to hear where they are now and what got them here. It's a conversation about change over the years. It might even feel easier than talking with the people we see every day, because we already know the stories of our current friends. With current friends, life is familiar, so it feels like there's not much to add. We're with them so much that we don't see the change happening. We only notice it when we look back and compare with the past.

All of us can think back to life events that caused sudden, radical change in the way we think and act. Those events stand out because they impacted us in a way that changed our trajectory moving forward. At the same time, it's easy to overlook the multitude of tiny events that tweak us in different directions.

190

We hear a sermon, get casual advice from a friend, gain insight while on a long run, or even find a change of perspective as we walk through a park. It causes us to think a little differently than we did before. Sometimes we notice the change, sometimes we don't. We're different every day because of the experiences of that day.

Though they are often imperceptible, those little inputs either make us better or worse, encouraged or discouraged. We become, over time, the sum of all of our choices about how we respond to the things that happen.

When we assume people haven't changed, we treat them exactly the same way we did the last time we talked to them. It doesn't matter if our last conversation was three days ago or thirty years ago; it was the last encounter we had, so we don't have any new input to tell us things are different.

Here's the problem: they've become a different person since the last time we talked, and so have we. To at least some degree, we're talking to a new person. If we don't take that into account, it can get in the way of effective communication.

Parents often do this with their grown children. Since they had them in their home for all of their formative years, they feel like they know their children better than anyone else— even after they've grown up and moved away. But once out of the parents' sight, children make their own choices regarding careers, relationships, and lifestyle. They develop an entire new network of friends and colleagues their parents have never met and know nothing about. Those experiences obviously shape them into different people than they were growing up at home. The parents don't see all of that, so they assume their children are handling their life situations the same way they did when they were at home.

I knew a father with a daughter in her midforties who had been in a great marriage for over twenty years. She and her husband were living on the other side of the country and had teenage children of their own. The father had a good relation-ship with his son-in-law but would often remark that he knew his daughter better than her husband did. "She was always stubborn," he would say when she expressed an opinion that was different from her husband's opinion. As a couple, they had learned skills of being open and honest in their commu-nication over the years, which made it safe to share their true feelings. But her dad hadn't experienced those changes and assumed she was only expressing the same stubbornness she had as a child.

What would happen to our relationships if we approached every conversation with curiosity about what was new? What if we thought, *I'm about to talk to someone I know who is now different than they were the last time we talked. I want to find out how they've changed.* Instead of just talking about the weather, we would have a sense of expectancy to learn more about where they are "in the moment."

It's easy to do this at a reunion because the changes are obvious. We expect people to be different. It's tougher with people we're around regularly, especially if we live with them. We think, *Of course I know them well; I see them every day!* But just as we have those brief moments that change the way we think, we never know when the other person has had a similar moment. They could've had a serious change in perspective, and we don't realize it.

That's worth exploring. It doesn't mean we bug our children by asking, "So, how are you different today?" It means we con-nect with them with the mindset that change is happening more than we realize (especially if they're teens). We're building a relationship by just walking with them on their own journey.

For example, say you had a conversation with your teenage son in which he shared his thoughts about some issue he was facing. He might have worked through it over the last few weeks and now has a totally different perspective on it. It probably

192

didn't occur to him to let you know of the change, so it's always good to avoid assumptions about what's really happening.

In such a case, you could let a month or so go by and then check in while you're having a comfortable conversation. "Hey, remember when we talked about that issue you were concerned about a few weeks ago? How are you feeling about it now?" Don't pry or push for details, just walk on the journey with him. If he wants to talk, he'll tell you. If he doesn't want to talk, he'll probably tell you about it when he's in his thirties.

Shaped by Change

Throughout our entire lives, it's a rare time when we're not changing. The rest of the time we're either getting better or worse. Life happens to all of us, and we become who we are by the way we respond to it.

When people are young, they generally welcome change. Sure, there are exceptions, but it's a time of anticipation. They don't want to stay the way they are and look for opportunities to grow and try something different. They see a lot of opportunity ahead of them, and it's exciting to explore the possibilities. They have hope for the future.

In midlife, positive change seems like a less realistic option because of the responsibilities that come with the season. People have bills to pay, kids to raise, jobs to keep, and relationships they're committed to. The only time change looks attractive is as an escape from being overwhelmed and overworked. People often feel trapped, and personal growth and impact are secondary to survival. They'd love to make some changes, but it feels unrealistic.

When they get older, there can be a sense of regret. They feel like they've made their choices and now they're stuck with the results. They've given up on change because it's easier just to accept their position in life. They're not as concerned about

193

changing the world as they are about changing their furniture arrangement. Wrinkles and routines become the norm, and people lose their sense of purpose. They think they're not changing, but they are daily—even if it's a slow, downward spiral toward becoming more cynical.

Think about who you are today compared to last month. You might not see huge changes, but you're still different. You've learned things you didn't know before. You have different perspectives because of the conversations you've had. You've read things, watched things, and listened to things that gradually made you a different person.

It's like rocks that have been highly polished in a tumbler; it doesn't happen overnight. The stones are put with some coarse grit in the tumbler, which turns day and night for a week or more to slowly remove the rough edges and smooth the stones. That's followed by another week in a medium grit, then finer and finer grit. You can never pull out a stone after two minutes and see anything different, but the changes are taking place.

In the same way, we become different people as the events in our lives slowly "polish" us. It happens to everyone but so slowly that it's easy to be unaware of the changes taking place. But just because we don't see it happening doesn't mean it's *not* happening.

Here's an exercise you can try today. Pay attention to everything that happens: the things you read, the conversations you have, the events that take place, and the random thoughts you have. Jot down anything that causes you to think differently or change your perspective. It doesn't have to be huge, just something that makes you go, *Hmm . . .*

At the end of the day, review the list and ask yourself, *So, with these thoughts, how am I different than I was this morning? How will I think differently going forward? How will my attitude be altered? How will my actions and choices be changed?*

194

In other words, *How will I be different tomorrow than I am today?* You'll probably be surprised at how the events of a single day can make you a changed person overnight. You start the new day from a slightly different place than you did yesterday.

You're a new person every day. You think differently, respond differently, and act differently. That means you communicate differently as well.

Intentional Conversations

Most of us go into conversations hoping for the best. We start the dialogue and see where it goes. Sometimes the conversation goes well; it's comfortable and enjoyable, and we simply share our thoughts. Other times it gets challenging, and we wish it had gone differently. Maybe we didn't have the courage to bring up something that needed to be discussed. Maybe we said things we wish we had left unsaid, and we have regrets later.

What if we went into our everyday conversations with the simple agenda of finding out how that person is different from the last time we talked to them? We don't have to get rigid and structured about our conversations. This is simply adding an intentional filter that lets us see what's new. Being *intentional* means we have something specific we're looking for. It involves listening carefully, then asking questions about what we hear to gain understanding.

When someone tells you about something they experienced or heard, go on a treasure hunt.

"Tell me more about that."

"What did that do inside your head when you heard it?"

"How is that changing your perspective?"

The big payoff is that every conversation becomes easier. Simple questions like these can give you new things to talk about as you gain clarity about what's changed for them. They'll feel listened to and understood, and this builds trust in the relationship. When there's trust, it is much easier to have the courage to bring up issues you might otherwise avoid.

In other words, the most important thing you can do to become courageous in conversations is to build trust in your relationships. That's not always possible, especially when you need to stand up for something in the moment, whether there's a relationship or not. But most of our daily conversations are with those we interact with frequently, and they're the people we want the most trust with.

It's a new paradigm—realizing that everyone changes every day. With my high school friends, we assume we're different people decades later. But we are different because we have become slightly altered every day over that time.

Redeeming the Reunion

When I think of the changes I see at my class reunions, there are a few factors I recognize that I'm able to apply to all of my relationships:

- Back then, we were sniffing out adulthood together. We were living at home but experimenting with the adult world for the first time. We wanted our curfew extended but wanted to be tucked in when we got home. We were changing every day, and we all knew it.
- We did life together. All of us were sticking our toes in the water of real life. We didn't know what we were doing, but we figured it out together. We were afraid to jump in but gained courage as we did it with friends. We had dreams and helped each other believe those dreams could come true. Our pursuit of those dreams changed us into different people.

196

- Once we jumped in, we began to move in different directions. We tried to stay connected after graduation but found our unique passions took us on individual paths. We weren't the people we used to be, but that was OK.
- We'll be forever bonded to the people we started the journey with. They have a special place in our hearts because we began the journey of change together, no matter where we each ended up.
- It's OK if we're not best friends anymore, because we're different people with different values and priorities. We were fellow travelers for a season, and we can always be grateful for the times and memories we had. Now, we've changed.
- Reunions give us a chance to be grateful for what those early relationships did for us, to hear each other's stories of change, and to celebrate our unique places in life.

After we have a reunion, we go our separate ways. But they give us a chance to talk about change—what we were like in those early days. We also get the chance to apologize for the unkind things we did in our adolescence (realizing we've grown out of that behavior—hopefully), affirm the value others brought into our lives, and move ahead better for it.

I miss my old friends. I wish we could be together this year. I don't care what they look like, how much they weigh, or what they've accomplished. I don't just want to see their picture in my yearbook. I want to hear their stories, grateful that we got to share a chunk of life together.

I want to learn how we've all changed, and how we'll be changing going forward.

They've changed. I've changed. *Isn't that awesome?*

If we embrace change, it can change everything!

The Last Word

Ready to Connect?

Throughout this book, we've looked at the challenges of conversations:

- Why it's so tough to speak up, and how to hold back for impact.
- How to become more assertive in a way that exactly matches our uniqueness.
- Learning to confront through deep caring.
- How to turn intimidation into confidence.
- The mechanics of successful communication.
- How to hone our skills through feedback and asking the right questions.
- Building new skills from scratch.
- Standing up for others.
- Becoming intentional to achieve specific outcomes any time we speak.

We could have looked at lists of tips and techniques for becoming more forceful and bold, but they won't work if they don't match who we really are. Instead, we've focused on ways to capitalize on our *uniqueness*—the most powerful resource we have to communicate with power. It's not a matter of copying what someone else does; it's about becoming the very best version of ourselves possible.

Confidence is achievable when the steps to get there are small enough. Take those steps consistently over time, and you'll be amazed at the skills you'll develop—skills no one else can do in the same way.

Are you ready to begin the journey?

Start by developing a clear vision of what you would like your communication to look like. Think carefully about the journey ahead. Go back through each chapter, working through them one by one for as long as needed until it becomes part of your toolkit.

The best part? If you take each step intentionally, you'll find joy in the journey. It won't be something tedious that feels impossible because it's so foreign to the way you've always been. You'll have the patience to see the steady growth, and you'll begin to believe you can make a serious difference in the world—simply by being *you*.

So, how are you going to stretch today? How will you use Brain One to learn or grow or make a difference, and Brain Two to make that change a lifestyle?

It's a great journey, and it's something you can begin right now!

Acknowledgments

Writing this section is always my favorite part of finishing a book. It's a chance to reflect on the people in my life who've been part of my journey leading up to the finished product, and to say thanks. It does good things in my head and heart to do it, because it's a reminder that writing is never a solo journey.

I put words together in isolation, but there's a whole army of people who have hung out with me and given me things of value to write about. Many of them are probably scared whenever we meet, because they know our conversations over coffee might end up in print. That's fairly accurate—not that I wrote down what they said, but because they made me think.

Glenn and Lana Meadows are in that category, as well as Paul and Vickie Gizzi and Ron and Linda Bishop. They're the people my wife and I do life with the most, so their care and concern helps shape who we are. We become progressively better people because of their intentional influence.

Jeremy Dorse is just simply my friend, and everybody needs one like him. He challenges me and believes in me. He's real, and it leaks into my life—and I write differently because of his influence.

Being part of the Portfolio People mastermind group has kept me grounded in the lives of fellow creatives, and we've been on this journey together. Jeff Goins called us together and invited us to quietly change the world with our words. In that context, it's easy to believe it's possible.

Then there's Vicki Crumpton, who has made me sound better than I do on my own for seven books now. It's refreshing to have a high-trust relationship with my editor and the confidence that my words are always safe in her hands. It's a dream partnership, and if she ever retires, you'll probably stop buying my books. She's that good.

I'm always amazed at how much influence my kids and grandkids have in my life. Sure, they're a joy to be around—but it's more than that. God often speaks almost audibly through their ideas and thoughts, and their fingerprints end up all over what I write. I've learned to listen deeply because they shape my world.

I wish I could find words to describe the sheer joy it is to be married to your best friend for forty-four years. It's partly because God has been so gracious to give Diane and me a true partnership. But it's also because we invest in that relationship and do the hard work of growing. We've always loved each other, and we still like each other too.

Then there's everybody I've ever met and talked to. Those connections fill me with feelings and thoughts that eventually come together in words. How grateful I am for everyday conversations with real people.

God has been there since the beginning, and that relationship shapes everything I do. I'm not sure what people do who don't know him, because I've experienced the reality of deep friendship with the Creator. He's not my religion; he's my life. He made me unique—which is the bottom line of this book.

So, to everybody . . . thanks. A lot.

I couldn't do it without you!

Notes

Part 1 The Case for Relevant Conversation

1. Mike Bechtle, *How to Communicate with Confidence* (Grand Rapids: Revell, 2012) and *Dealing with the Elephant in the Room: Moving from Tough Conversations to Healthy Communication* (Grand Rapids: Revell, 2015).

Chapter 1 Making a Dent

1. John Maxwell, *Failing Forward: Turning Mistakes into Stepping Stones for Success* (Nashville: HarperCollins Leadership, 2007).
2. "Psychological Resilience," Wikipedia, accessed July 20, 2021, https://en.wikipedia.org/wiki/Psychological_resilience#cite_note-1.

Chapter 2 What's Holding You Back?

1. Judith E. Glaser, "Why We Don't Speak Up," *Psychology Today*, May 22, 2018, https://www.psychologytoday.com/us/blog/conversational-intelligence/201805/why-we-don-t-speak.

Chapter 3 Your Temperament Is Your Superpower

1. Brian Resnick, "If You're Just Not a Morning Person, Science Says You May Never Be," *Vox*, March 17, 2017, https://www.vox.com/2016/3/18/11255942/morning-people-evening-chronotypes-sleeping.
2. John Ortberg, *The Me I Want to Be: Becoming God's Best Version of You* (Grand Rapids: Zondervan, 2009), 16.
3. The Beatles, "Let It Be," lyrics by Paul McCartney and John Lennon, from the album *Let It Be* (London: Apple Records, 1970).

Chapter 4 Confrontation, Not Conflict

1. "Confront," Lexico, accessed July 20, 2021, https://www.lexico.com/en/definition/confront.

2. Rory Vaden, *Take the Stairs: 7 Steps to Achieving True Success* (New York: Penguin Group, 2012), 34.

3. David Augsburger, "Quote of the Day," Good News Network, October 27, 2019, https://www.goodnewsnetwork.org/david-augsburger-quote-on-being-heard/.

Chapter 8 Feelings as Fuel

1. William Shakespeare, *The Tragedy of Hamlet, Prince of Denmark*, act 2, scene 2, http://shakespeare.mit.edu/hamlet/hamlet.2.2.html.

2. Max Lucado, *Anxious for Nothing: Finding Calm in a Chaotic World* (Nashville: HarperCollins, 2017), 121.

3. "Attitude," *The Oxford Pocket Dictionary of Current English*, accessed July 20, 2021, https://www.encyclopedia.com/humanities/dictionaries-thesauruses-pictures-and-press-releases/attitude-0.

4. This appears to be a widely quoted compilation of smaller quotes by Swindoll. See, for example, Laurie Baedke, "Sunny Side Up: Having an Attitude That Shines," *Laurie Baedke*, accessed July 20, 2021, http://www.choosingvoluntarysimplicity.com/the-impact-of-attitude-on-life/.

5. James Allen, "James Allen Quotes," Ask Ideas, accessed June 15, 2021, https://www.askideas.com/every-action-and-feeling-is-preceded-by-a-thought/.

6. John Maxwell, "Quotable Quotes," Goodreads, accessed June 15, 2021, https://www.goodreads.com/quotes/1309491-fail-early-fail-often-but-always-fail-forward.

Chapter 9 The Power of Silence

1. Susan Scott, *Fierce Conversations: Achieving Success at Work and in Life, One Conversation at a Time* (New York: Penguin Random House, 2004), 278.

2. Mark Twain, "Quotable Quotes," Goodreads, accessed June 15, 2021, https://www.goodreads.com/quotes/21422-i-didn-t-have-time-to-write-a-short-letter-so.

3. Friedrich Nietzsche, "Skirmishes in a War with the Age," section 51, in *The Twilight of the Idols*, accessed June 10, 2021, https://www.gutenberg.org/files/52263/52263-h/52263-h.htm.

4. Richard B. Joelson, "Silence in a Relationship," Richard B. Joelson, accessed June 15, 2021, https://richardbjoelsondsw.com/articles/silence-in-a-relationship/.

Chapter 10 How to Change Someone's Mind

1. Eric Barker, "This Is How to Change Someone's Mind: 6 Secrets from Research," *Barking Up the Wrong Tree* (blog), accessed June 15, 2021, https://www.bakadesuyo.com/2019/12/change-someones-mind/.

Chapter 13 Being Humble without Being Weak

1. Mel Schwartz, "Why Acting Strong Is Really Weak," *Psychology Today*, February 25, 2016, https://www.psychologytoday.com/us/blog/shift-mind /201602/why-acting-strong-is-really-weak.

2. Mac Davis, "It's Hard to Be Humble Lyrics," Lyrics.com, accessed June 15, 2021, https://www.lyrics.com/lyric/29338816/Mac+Davis/It%27s +Hard+to+Be+Humble.

Chapter 14 How to Speak Up for Others

1. Jim Rohn, "Official Jim Rohn Facebook page," posted May 30, 2014, https://www.facebook.com/OfficialJimRohn/posts/success-lies-in-the-op posite-direction-of-the-normal-pull-jim-rohn/10154170957100635/.

2. "Quotes: *The Legend of Bagger Vance* (2000)," Quotes.net, accessed June 15, 2021, https://www.quotes.net/mquote/1101708.

Chapter 15 Getting Feedback

1. Carol Dweck, *Mindset: The New Psychology of Success* (New York: Ballantine, 2007).

2. Ken Blanchard, "Feedback Is the Breakfast of Champions," Facebook video, 0:50, posted February 3, 2021, https://www.facebook.com/watch /?v=234823064889901.

Dr. Mike Bechtle (EdD, Arizona State University) is the author of seven books, including *People Can't Drive You Crazy If You Don't Give Them the Keys* and *How to Communicate with Confidence*. His articles have appeared in publications such as *Writer's Digest*, Pastors.com, and *Entrepreneur*. A frequent speaker and media guest, Bechtle lives in California. Learn more at www.mikebechtle.com.

FOR MORE
COMMUNICATION TOOLS,
PRACTICAL
INSIGHT,
AND MOTIVATION, VISIT

MIKEBECHTLE.COM

  @MIKEBECHTLE

Discover More Resources from Mike

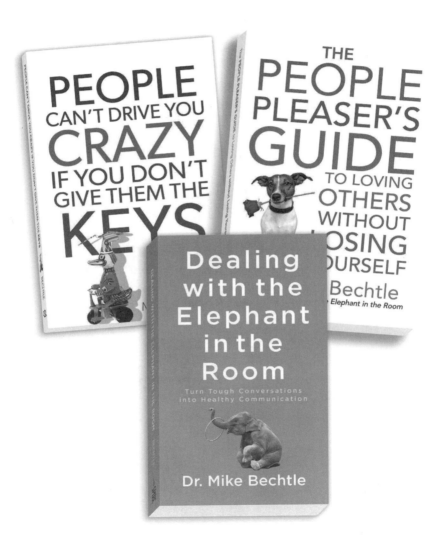